KT-555-232

Collins

SNAP REVISION

DR JEKYLL AND MR HYDE

AQA GCSE English Literature

IAN KIRBY

REVISE SET TEXTS IN A SNAP

Published by Collins
An imprint of HarperCollinsPublishers
1 London Bridge Street,
London, SE1 9GF

© HarperCollinsPublishers Limited 2017

9780008247102

First published 2017

10 9 8 7 6 5 4 3

All rights reserved. No part of this publication
may be reproduced, stored in a retrieval system,
or transmitted, in any form or by any means,
electronic, mechanical, photocopying, recording or
otherwise, without the prior permission of Collins.

British Library Cataloguing in Publication Data.

A CIP record of this book is available from the
British Library.

Printed in the Italy by Grafica Veneta S.p.A

Commissioning Editor: Gillian Bowman
Managing Editor: Craig Balfour
Author: Ian Kirby
Copyeditor: David Christie
Proofreaders: Jill Laidlaw and Louise Robb
Project management and typesetting:
  Mark Steward
Cover designers: Kneath Associates and
  Sarah Duxbury
Production: Natalia Rebow

ACKNOWLEDGEMENTS

The author and publisher are grateful to the
copyright holders for permission to use quoted
materials and images.

Every effort has been made to trace copyright
holders and obtain their permission for the use of
copyright material. The author and publisher will
gladly receive information enabling them to rectify
any error or omission in subsequent editions. All
facts are correct at time of going to press.

HarperCollins
PUBLISHERS
Since 1817

Contents

Chapter 1

You must be able to: understand what happens in 'Story of the Door'.

Who are the first characters that are introduced?

Stevenson begins the novel by describing Mr Utterson, a lawyer. He is a serious man with strong values who cares for others.

Stevenson contrasts Mr Utterson with Mr Richard Enfield, a distant relative who is wealthy, popular and fashionable.

Despite their differences, they meet every Sunday for a walk.

How is the plot introduced?

Stevenson describes the two men walking along a side-street in a busy part of London.

A sinister, neglected-looking building is introduced and Mr Enfield draws Mr Utterson's attention to it, saying he has a strange story relating to the door of the building.

Mr Enfield then describes how he was returning home in the early hours of the morning when he saw a small man and a young girl knock into each other by accident. However, instead of helping the girl, the man ran over her body.

This is Mr Hyde but, at this point in the story, Stevenson leaves him unnamed.

Mr Enfield goes on to say how he apprehended the man and brought him back to the girl, where her family had gathered. A doctor – who Mr Enfield refers to as 'the Sawbones' – was called and the girl was fine, just frightened.

How is mystery introduced to the story?

Mr Enfield continues his narrative, explaining that he disliked the small man and was surprised to find that the doctor appeared to hate him as well. They threatened to cause a scandal that would bring the small man into disrepute unless he paid the family some compensation.

The man agreed, went into the sinister building and returned with a cheque. Mr Enfield and the doctor were suspicious because the cheque was signed by someone else. He is surprised when the bank says the cheque is genuine and the money is paid.

This refers to Dr Jekyll but, again, at this point, Stevenson doesn't reveal his name to the reader.

Mr Enfield finishes his story by suggesting that the owner of the house is being blackmailed by the small man.

Mr Utterson asks further questions about the story and Mr Enfield reveals that the small man's name was Mr Hyde and that he looked strange and loathsome.

Mr Utterson admits to being uncomfortable; he discloses that he knows something of the story already, including who owns the building that Mr Hyde entered. He doesn't go into any more detail and the two men agree not to discuss the story again.

Key Quotations to Learn

'It is connected in my mind,' added he, 'with a very odd story.' (Mr Enfield)

'... every time he looked at my prisoner, I saw that Sawbones turn sick and white with desire to kill him.' (Mr Enfield)

Mr Utterson again walked some way in silence and obviously under a weight of consideration.

Summary

- Despite being quite different, Mr Utterson and Mr Enfield are close friends.
- On one of their walks, Mr Enfield points out the door of a building and describes his encounter with Mr Hyde.
- He saw Mr Hyde knock over a young girl and describes him as a small, strange, violent and hateful man.
- He thinks the owner of the building is being blackmailed by Mr Hyde.
- Mr Utterson knows more about the story than he wants to reveal, and he and his friend agree not to talk about it again.

Questions

QUICK TEST
1. What is noticeable about the building with the door?
2. What horrible thing did Mr Enfield see Mr Hyde do?
3. What reaction do Mr Enfield and the doctor both have towards Mr Hyde?
4. Why do Mr Enfield and the doctor think Mr Hyde is blackmailing the owner of the building?
5. Which important character isn't actually named in Chapter 1 and why?

EXAM PRACTICE
Using one or more of the 'Key Quotations to Learn', write a paragraph analysing how Stevenson establishes a sense of mystery in Chapter 1.

Chapters 2 and 3

You must be able to: understand what happens in 'Search for Mr Hyde' and 'Dr Jekyll Was Quite at Ease'.

What does Mr Utterson know about Mr Hyde and Dr Jekyll?

Stevenson describes Mr Utterson returning home, clearly disturbed by Mr Enfield's story.

Because he is Dr Henry Jekyll's lawyer, he has a copy of his will. It states that all of his possessions will go to Mr Edward Hyde should he disappear for more than three months or die.

Now he has found out what Mr Hyde is like, Mr Utterson is very suspicious of the terms of the will.

Needing someone to discuss the matter with, he goes to see his old friend, Dr Lanyon. However, the doctor has not seen their mutual friend for years and he angrily describes Dr Jekyll as 'fanciful' and 'unscientific'. He has never heard of Edward Hyde.

How does Mr Utterson become more involved?

Mr Utterson returns home to sleep but has a nightmare about Mr Hyde.

He decides that he wants to meet Mr Hyde and begins to wait around near the door that Mr Enfield pointed out.

When he finally meets Mr Hyde, he is troubled by his ugly, almost inhuman appearance. Mr Hyde behaves in a rude and secretive way, losing his temper when Mr Utterson lies that he heard about him from Dr Jekyll.

He is worried about his friend so he goes around the corner to the front of the house but is told by Poole, the manservant, that Dr Jekyll has gone out. He finds out that Mr Hyde often visits the house from the back entrance, spending time in Dr Jekyll's laboratory.

Mr Utterson returns home but is still concerned and decides that he will try to help Dr Jekyll.

How does Stevenson introduce Dr Jekyll?

Stevenson moves the narrative on by a fortnight to an evening dinner at Dr Jekyll's house. Mr Utterson waits until the other guests have gone and then mentions the will.

Dr Jekyll remains calm but he is clearly uncomfortable talking about the will. When Mr Utterson reveals that he has been finding things out about Mr Hyde, Dr Jekyll tries to end the conversation.

Mr Utterson says he can help but Dr Jekyll reassures him that there is nothing wrong: he says he cares about Mr Hyde but could 'be rid of' him if he wanted to. He asks Mr Utterson to promise that the terms of the will shall be followed correctly and Mr Hyde will inherit everything.

Mr Utterson reluctantly agrees.

Key Quotations to Learn

… he replaced the obnoxious paper in the safe, 'and now I begin to fear it is disgrace.' (Mr Utterson about the will: Chapter 2)

'It turns me cold to think of this creature stealing like a thief to Harry's bedside; poor Harry,' (Mr Utterson: Chapter 2)

Utterson heaved an irrepressible sigh. 'Well,' said he, 'I promise.'(Chapter 3)

Summary

- Mr Utterson looks at Dr Jekyll's will: if he vanishes for more than three months or dies, Mr Hyde inherits everything.
- Mr Utterson visits an old friend, Dr Lanyon, and it appears he and Dr Jekyll have fallen out after a scientific disagreement.
- Mr Utterson decides to meet Mr Hyde but, when he does, he becomes more concerned by the dislikeable man.
- He offers to help Dr Jekyll but his friend tells him there is no need for concern.

Questions

QUICK TEST
1. How does Dr Jekyll's will make Mr Utterson feel?
2. How does Dr Lanyon react when Mr Utterson tries to discuss Dr Jekyll with him?
3. How does Mr Hyde behave towards Mr Utterson when they meet?
4. What does Mr Hyde get angry about?
5. To reassure Mr Utterson about his relationship with Edward Hyde, what does Dr Jekyll say he can do?

EXAM PRACTICE
Using one or more of the 'Key Quotations to Learn', write a paragraph analysing how Stevenson shows that Mr Utterson is worried about Dr Jekyll.

Chapters 4 to 6

You must be able to: understand what happens in 'The Carew Murder Case', 'Incident of the Letter' and 'Incident of Dr Lanyon'.

Who does Mr Hyde murder?

Stevenson moves the narrative on by a year to the murder of Sir Danvers Carew.

A woman saw Carew walking down the street where he encounters Mr Hyde, who suddenly beats Carew with a cane and then stamps on his body.

Mr Utterson is contacted because a letter addressed to him was found on the body. He goes to the police station and identifies the dead man. Mr Utterson also recognises the murder weapon as a cane that he gave to Dr Jekyll.

He and the police go to Mr Hyde's lodgings in a run-down part of London. He isn't there but they inspect his rooms and Mr Utterson is surprised by how nice they are compared to Mr Hyde himself.

The main room has been ransacked, papers have been burned, and the other half of the murder weapon is discovered. The police begin searching for the fugitive.

How does Dr Jekyll react to the news of the murder?

The same day, Mr Utterson goes to see Dr Jekyll. He looks ill and scared. He has heard about the murder and promises never to see Mr Hyde again. He shows Mr Utterson a letter from Mr Hyde that was hand-delivered to the house, stating he has made his escape.

On his way out, Mr Utterson discovers that no post had been delivered that day. Later, at his office, Mr Utterson's head clerk, Mr Guest, points out that Mr Hyde's handwriting is the same as Dr Jekyll's, just at a different angle.

Mr Utterson is shocked by the idea that Dr Jekyll might be helping to hide a murderer.

How does Stevenson begin to link Dr Jekyll and Dr Lanyon?

Stevenson moves the narrative forward again, describing how Mr Hyde is never discovered and, without his influence, Dr Jekyll becomes more sociable again.

However, Dr Jekyll suddenly stops accepting visitors and refuses to see Mr Utterson.

Mr Utterson visits Dr Lanyon to see if he knows what is wrong but finds him terribly ill. He says that he has suffered a bad shock and becomes distressed when Dr Jekyll is mentioned.

Mr Utterson tries contacting Dr Jekyll again and receives a letter, asking to be left alone.

Dr Lanyon dies a fortnight later. Mr Utterson receives an envelope, written by Dr Lanyon before his death, with the strange instruction that is it not to be opened until the death or disappearance of Dr Jekyll.

Key Quotations to Learn

… there, close up to the warmth, sat Dr Jekyll, looking deathly sick. (Chapter 5)

'What!' he thought. 'Henry Jekyll forge for a murderer!' And his blood ran cold in his veins. (Mr Utterson: Chapter 5)

Now that the evil influence had been withdrawn, a new life began for Dr Jekyll. (Chapter 6)

Summary

- After viciously murdering Sir Danvers Carew, Mr Hyde disappears.
- Mr Utterson worries that Dr Jekyll may be covering up for Mr Hyde.
- After Mr Hyde's disappearance, Dr Jekyll becomes more sociable again.
- However, one day he returns to his secretive ways and refuses to see anyone.
- Mr Utterson discovers that Dr Lanyon is ill. He says he has had a terrible shock and dies a fortnight later.
- Mr Utterson then receives an envelope from Dr Lanyon that is not to be opened until after the death or disappearance of Dr Jekyll.

Questions

QUICK TEST
1. What details about the murder of Sir Danvers Carew made it particularly vicious?
2. What is surprising about Mr Hyde's lodgings?
3. Why does Mr Utterson suspect Dr Jekyll may be shielding Mr Hyde?
4. What two things does Stevenson add to the story to link Dr Jekyll and Dr Lanyon?

EXAM PRACTICE
Using one or more of the 'Key Quotations to Learn', write a paragraph analysing how Stevenson suggests how Dr Jekyll is affected by the murder of Danvers Carew.

Chapters 7 and 8

You must be able to: understand what happens in 'Incident at the Window' and 'The Last Night'.

How does Dr Jekyll's behaviour become more suspicious?

On one of their Sunday walks, Mr Utterson and Mr Enfield pass by Dr Jekyll's house and see him sitting at the window. They call up to him and he tells them that he is very unhappy.

Part way through their conversation, Dr Jekyll's face suddenly fills with horror before he closes the window and disappears from sight. Both men are shocked by what they have witnessed.

What does Poole believe has happed to Dr Jekyll?

Some time later, Mr Utterson is visited one evening by Dr Jekyll's manservant, Poole. He looks scared, says Dr Jekyll has locked himself in the laboratory, and fears 'foul play'.

Mr Utterson agrees to go to the house with Poole. They go to the laboratory where Poole calls through the door to Dr Jekyll. Listening to the reply, Poole explains to Mr Utterson that it isn't Dr Jekyll's voice.

He explains that eight days ago he heard Dr Jekyll cry out in the laboratory and, since then, someone else has remained locked in the laboratory. He believes Dr Jekyll has been murdered.

Poole explains how, for the last week, the person in the laboratory has been crying out for medicine and sending him to a chemist to collect a certain drug. He retells how, returning from the chemist, he once found the laboratory door open and saw a small, strange man who cried out and ran back into the room. He is sure that it was Mr Hyde.

They listen through the door to someone walking back and forth in the laboratory. Mr Utterson calls to Dr Jekyll but recognises the voice that replies as Mr Hyde's. He orders Poole to break down the door with an axe.

What do they find in Dr Jekyll's laboratory?

They hear a scream from the laboratory and, after breaking in, find Mr Hyde dying on the floor. He appears to be wearing the larger clothes of Dr Jekyll and he has poisoned himself. There is no sign of Dr Jekyll.

On a table, they find an envelope addressed to Mr Utterson. Inside are several documents and a note from Dr Jekyll. The note tells him to read the document sent to him by Dr Lanyon and to then read his own enclosed confession.

Utterson returns home to read the two documents in the hope of understanding the mysterious events.

Key Quotations to Learn

... Mr Enfield only nodded his head very seriously and walked on once more in silence. (Chapter 7)

'... he's shut up again in the cabinet; and I don't like it, sir – I wish I may die if I like it. Mr Utterson, sir, I'm afraid.' (Poole: Chapter 8)

'Sir,' said the butler, turning to a sort of mottled pallor, 'that thing was not my master,' (Chapter 8)

Summary

- Poole visits Mr Utterson, worried that his master, Dr Jekyll, has been murdered by Mr Hyde.
- He has not heard Dr Jekyll's voice for over a week but someone is still in the laboratory pretending to be him and asking for drugs from the chemist.
- Mr Utterson goes to Dr Jekyll's house. When they hear Mr Hyde's voice, Poole breaks down the door of the laboratory.
- Before they can get inside, Mr Hyde poisons himself. There is no sign of Dr Jekyll but there is a letter from him, addressed to Mr Utterson.

Questions

QUICK TEST
1. What strange behaviour of Dr Jekyll's did Mr Utterson and Mr Enfield witness?
2. Why does Poole think Dr Jekyll has been murdered?
3. As well as hearing him, why does Poole think it is Mr Hyde in the laboratory?
4. What do they find in the laboratory?

EXAM PRACTICE
Using one or more of the 'Key Quotations to Learn', write a paragraph analysing how Stevenson creates an **ominous atmosphere**.

Chapter 9

You must be able to: understand what happens in 'Dr Lanyon's Narrative'.

How does the novel change?

Stevenson moves the story back in time to a few weeks before Dr Lanyon's death. The narrative has also shifted from a **third-person narrative** to a **first-person narrative**, written to Mr Utterson from Dr Lanyon's perspective.

Dr Lanyon describes how he was surprised to receive a letter one evening from Dr Jekyll. The letter is then included as part of the narrative.

Dr Jekyll writes that he and Dr Lanyon have had a scientific disagreement but says that he would always have helped him in an emergency. He then asks for Dr Lanyon's help. The letter requests that he goes to Dr Jekyll's laboratory, where Poole is waiting with a locksmith. After breaking into the laboratory, Dr Lanyon should collect certain chemicals and take them back to his own house. He is told that someone will then call at midnight and that this person should be given the chemicals.

What events does Dr Lanyon describe?

Dr Lanyon then writes how he presumed Dr Jekyll was mad but followed his instructions. Retelling the collection of the chemicals from Dr Jekyll's laboratory, he comments on an unusual notebook that showed experiments with different quantities of mixtures.

He continues to describe how, at midnight, a small man visited the house. The reader will guess that this is Mr Hyde but Dr Lanyon does not use his name. He is suspicious of the man and repulsed by him, mentioning his strange facial appearance and the fact that his clothes were far too big for him.

The small man is desperate for the chemicals. When they are handed over, he begins to mix a potion. He asks Dr Lanyon if he would prefer to watch him drink the potion or if he would prefer him to leave the house and drink it, warning him that to watch will reveal new and terrible knowledge.

Dr Lanyon tells the man to drink it in front of him. He does so and Dr Lanyon describes his horror as the man goes through a painful physical transformation and becomes Dr Jekyll.

He finishes his narrative by writing that Dr Jekyll spent the next hour giving him a full explanation that appalled him. He won't repeat what he was told but feels that the shock of the evening has brought him close to death. In his last sentence, he confirms that the small man was Mr Hyde, the murderer of Sir Danvers Carew.

Upon the reading of this letter, I made sure my colleague was insane;

(... from the first moment of his entrance, struck in me what I can only describe as a disgustful curiosity)

... groping before him with his hands, like a man restored from death – there stood Henry Jekyll!

Summary

- The novel becomes a first-person narrative, written to Mr Utterson from Dr Lanyon's perspective.
- He includes a letter he received one night from Dr Jekyll, asking for his help.
- After collecting chemicals from Dr Jekyll's laboratory, he is visited at midnight by Mr Hyde.
- Before his eyes, Mr Hyde mixes and drinks a potion that transforms him back into Dr Jekyll.
- Dr Lanyon is horrified by the events and shocked to realise the double identity of the man who murdered Sir Danvers Carew.

Questions

QUICK TEST
1. How is this chapter written differently to the previous eight chapters?
2. What conclusion did Dr Lanyon make about Dr Jekyll after reading his letter?
3. What did Dr Lanyon find strange about the man who arrives at his house at midnight?
4. Before drinking the potion, what choice does Mr Hyde give to Dr Lanyon?
5. How does Dr Lanyon feel the night's events have affected him?

EXAM PRACTICE
Using one or more of the 'Key Quotations to Learn', write a paragraph analysing how Stevenson conveys Dr Lanyon's feelings about Dr Jekyll and/or Mr Hyde.

You must be able to: understand what happens in 'Henry Jekyll's Full Statement of the Case'.

Why did Dr Jekyll create Mr Hyde?

Dr Jekyll describes having a wealthy family and how his wish to enjoy life conflicted with his wish to have others respect him, leading to him hiding many of his pleasures.

He explains his belief that people have two sides: one controlled and moral, the other instinctual and corrupt. He began to explore this **duality** through his scientific studies. Eventually, he experimented on himself, drinking a potion that turned him into a younger, happier, but more immoral man. Using another potion, he could change back into Henry Jekyll.

He started to use the potion to transform himself into Mr Hyde, in order to enjoy himself in a way that he couldn't as Dr Jekyll without harming his reputation.

How did Mr Hyde become a problem?

He loved the freedom that being Mr Hyde allowed him but his pleasures became increasingly depraved.

One morning, he woke up to find that he had transformed into Mr Hyde in his sleep, without using the potion, suggesting Mr Hyde was becoming the dominant side of his personality.

He decided to continue his life only as Dr Jekyll but eventually gave into temptation and drank the potion again. The Mr Hyde that emerged was much wilder than before and murdered Sir Danvers Carew.

Realising he could never be Mr Hyde again, he focussed on using his medical skills to help others and began to live a more fulfilled life. However, one day he changed involuntarily into Mr Hyde.

Now in the form of a wanted murderer, he had to go into hiding and call on Dr Lanyon's help to get him the drugs he needed to change back. The unwanted transformation into Mr Hyde took place again the following day and, this time, a double dose of the drug was needed and it only lasted six hours.

The Mr Hyde side of his personality was increasingly powerful and monstrous. He began to run out of the drug needed to transform back and when he bought a new supply it didn't have the same effect.

In the last paragraph of the novel, Dr Jekyll finishes his confession. He has run out of the original drug and knows that the next time he changes he won't be able to change back. He wonders whether Mr Hyde will be caught and hanged by the police or whether he will commit suicide.

Key Quotations to Learn

There was something strange in my sensations, something indescribably new and, from its very novelty, incredibly sweet.

... my blood was changed into something exquisitely thin and icy. Yes, I had gone to bed Henry Jekyll, I had awakened Edward Hyde.

He, I say – I cannot say I. That child of Hell had nothing human;

Summary

- The final chapter is told from Dr Jekyll's perspective.
- He explains how he created Mr Hyde out of his belief that people have two sides to their character: one good and one bad.
- Mr Hyde allowed him to do bad things that he couldn't do as the respectable Dr Jekyll.
- However, Mr Hyde became more powerful and Dr Jekyll couldn't stop himself from changing into him.
- Having run out of the necessary drug, Dr Jekyll realises that the next time he changes into Mr Hyde he won't be able to change back.

Questions

QUICK TEST
1. What does Dr Jekyll manage to maintain by only doing the bad things that he enjoys when in the shape of Mr Hyde?
2. What happens that suggests Mr Hyde is becoming the dominant side of Dr Jekyll's personality?
3. Why does changing from Mr Hyde back into Dr Jekyll become increasingly difficult?
4. At the very end of the novel, in what way is Dr Jekyll about to die?

EXAM PRACTICE
Using two or more of the 'Key Quotations to Learn', write a paragraph analysing how Stevenson presents Dr Jekyll's changing attitude towards Mr Hyde.

Narrative Form and Structure

You must be able to: understand the different effects of the ways Stevenson has shaped and structured the novel.

What form of narrator is used?

The story is told through multiple narrators; this is called multiperspectivity.

The first half of the novel features a third-person **omniscient** narrator, telling of Mr Utterson's involvement in the story (although much of the first chapter is Mr Enfield's direct speech).

In Chapter 9, Stevenson shifts to a first-person narrator, Dr Lanyon, in the form of a letter sent to Mr Utterson. This chapter also contains a letter written by Dr Jekyll.

The final chapter remains in the first person but is this time narrated by Dr Jekyll in the form of a confession left for Mr Utterson.

How is the narrative structured?

The first chapter features a **flashback**, through Mr Enfield's speech, to introduce the character of Mr Hyde. The remainder of the first half of the novel is a **linear narrative**, with events told in the order in which they happened.

The last two chapters create a non-linear narrative. Chapter 9 takes the story back several months to explain Dr Lanyon's death and reveal the truth of Dr Jekyll/Mr Hyde. Chapter 10 takes the story back to Henry Jekyll's birth and then features the key events that led up to Mr Utterson's discovery of Mr Hyde's dead body at the end of Chapter 8.

How does Stevenson keep the reader engaged?

Stevenson uses the third-person linear narrative to establish character, plot and setting, hooking the reader with a series of strange, unexplained events.

He controls what the reader knows: giving details that create **tension** or excitement, and withholding information to create mystery. Cliffhangers are used at the end of most chapters (in particular chapters 2, 4, 5 and 8) to create suspense for the reader.

The change to first-person narration is used by Stevenson to create horror whilst resolving the story and raising questions about humanity and **morality**. Terror is heightened through the immediacy of Dr Lanyon's first-hand experience of the transformation; Dr Jekyll's confession adds motivation and explanation of the events, allowing the reader to understand his conflicting feelings and moral dilemmas.

Like many Victorian novels that feature horror or the supernatural, the first-person narrators are intelligent, rational scientists with social status. This, alongside seemingly authentic forms like letters, was used to add a sense of reliability and believability so readers would find the story scarier.

Key Quotations to Learn

For once more he saw before his mind's eye, as clear as transparency, the strange clauses of the will. (Chapter 2)

My life is shaken to its roots; sleep has left me; the deadliest terror sits by me at all hours of the day and night; (Dr Lanyon: Chapter 9)

... the course of my scientific discoveries had begun to suggest the most naked possibility of such a miracle, (Dr Jekyll: Chapter 10)

Summary

- Stevenson uses multiple narrators to achieve different effects.
- Each chapter is told in a linear way but the novel's overall narrative structure is non-linear.
- He uses the third person to establish the plot and engage the reader, creating mystery and tension through the withholding of information and inclusion of cliffhangers.
- He then heightens the horror while resolving the story through the first person, adding depth to the novel by raising questions about human nature.

Questions

QUICK TEST
1. In what way is the first chapter not wholly written in the third person?
2. Which other chapters feature a third-person omniscient narrator?
3. What features of narrative structure does Stevenson use to keep the reader engaged?
4. Who are the two first-person narrators?
5. What does Stevenson bring to the novel through his use of the first person?

EXAM PRACTICE
Using one or more of the 'Key Quotations to Learn', write a paragraph analysing how Stevenson uses narrative structure and/or form to engage the reader.

Timeline of Events

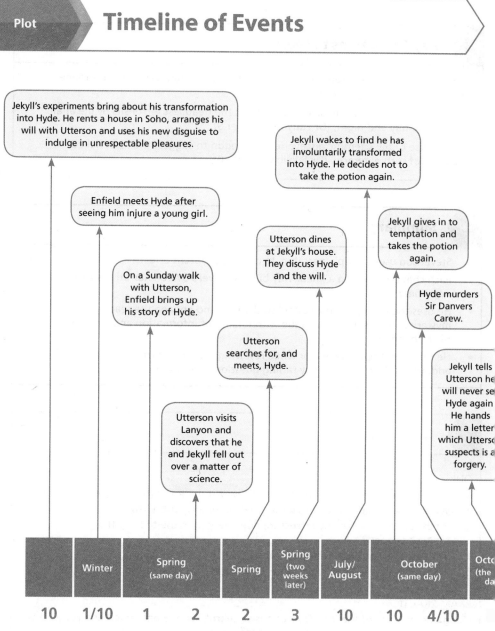

Jekyll's experiments bring about his transformation into Hyde. He rents a house in Soho, arranges his will with Utterson and uses his new disguise to indulge in unrespectable pleasures.

Enfield meets Hyde after seeing him injure a young girl.

On a Sunday walk with Utterson, Enfield brings up his story of Hyde.

Utterson searches for, and meets, Hyde.

Utterson visits Lanyon and discovers that he and Jekyll fell out over a matter of science.

Utterson dines at Jekyll's house. They discuss Hyde and the will.

Jekyll wakes to find he has involuntarily transformed into Hyde. He decides not to take the potion again.

Jekyll gives in to temptation and takes the potion again.

Hyde murders Sir Danvers Carew.

Jekyll tells Utterson he will never see Hyde again. He hands him a letter which Utterson suspects is a forgery.

	Winter	Spring (same day)	Spring	Spring (two weeks later)	July/ August	October (same day)	Octo (the da
10	1/10	1	2	2	3	10	10	4/10

Chapter

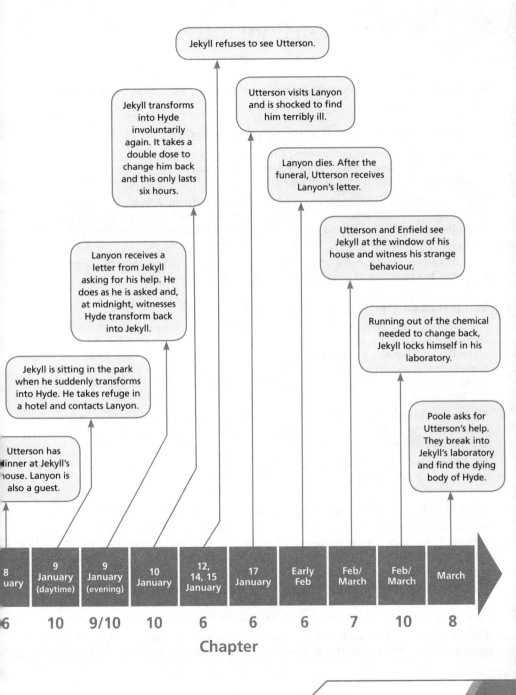

Jekyll refuses to see Utterson.

Jekyll transforms into Hyde involuntarily again. It takes a double dose to change him back and this only lasts six hours.

Utterson visits Lanyon and is shocked to find him terribly ill.

Lanyon dies. After the funeral, Utterson receives Lanyon's letter.

Lanyon receives a letter from Jekyll asking for his help. He does as he is asked and, at midnight, witnesses Hyde transform back into Jekyll.

Utterson and Enfield see Jekyll at the window of his house and witness his strange behaviour.

Jekyll is sitting in the park when he suddenly transforms into Hyde. He takes refuge in a hotel and contacts Lanyon.

Running out of the chemical needed to change back, Jekyll locks himself in his laboratory.

Utterson has dinner at Jekyll's house. Lanyon is also a guest.

Poole asks for Utterson's help. They break into Jekyll's laboratory and find the dying body of Hyde.

8 uary	9 January (daytime)	9 January (evening)	10 January	12, 14, 15 January	17 January	Early Feb	Feb/ March	Feb/ March	March
6	10	9/10	10	6	6	6	7	10	8

Chapter

You must be able to: understand how the novel reflects what England was like in the nineteenth century.

What social problems did the country have?

Stevenson's novel is set in nineteenth-century London. The cities of England – particularly the capital – contained a lot of poverty and homelessness. There were areas of awful squalor with poor living conditions and disease.

There was a lack of equality for the working classes, especially women. This included a lack of education. Because there weren't enough jobs for the number of people living in the cities, these people often found it difficult to survive. If people were too ill or too old to work, there was no social care; they were just left without money.

This all led to a rise in crime and prostitution. Due to increased trade with foreign countries, the new **vice** of drug abuse also began to grow.

What had caused these problems?

The Industrial Revolution, which began in the second half of the eighteenth century, created new manufacturing processes that led to large factories being built in the major cities. England became a mass producer of steel, iron, textiles, paper and chemicals. Smaller manufacturers couldn't compete and closed down so many people moved to the cities, looking for work. Industrialisation made some people very rich, creating what is now called the middle class.

Governments were also to blame for not spending enough money quickly enough on making the cities suitable for the growing populations. Politicians were upper class so they often didn't care enough for the sufferings of the working class.

The Church was also criticised. Although it had a much more significant role in society and politics than it does today, it did little to help people in need.

How does Stevenson explore these problems in the novel?

Published in 1886, the novel presents an image of wealthy, professional people living in London. They either condemn or ignore the poverty, vice and suffering that was rife at the time. This is the kind of life that many of Stevenson's readers would have known and he criticises this social attitude.

Through Jekyll's transformation into Hyde, the reader is forced to see the underbelly of city life in England. It is also made clear that problems such as drug abuse and prostitution partly exist because wealthy people like Jekyll spend their money on these vices.

Stevenson doesn't focus on how these problems should be solved. Instead, he explores why people indulge in vice, and asserts that it cannot be ignored or simply blamed on others.

Summary

- Victorian England was growing wealthy through industrialisation but its cities were also full of poverty.
- Crime, drug abuse and prostitution were increasing problems in major cities.
- The rich tended to ignore the country's problems while some indulged in the criminal vice that was available.
- Stevenson was interested in revealing these problems to his readers, not because he had a solution but because it was a reality that couldn't be ignored or blamed on others.

Questions

QUICK TEST

1. What source of income did many women turn to if they were struggling to survive?
2. What vice was growing in the major cities due to trade with other countries?
3. What two sections of the establishment were blamed for not doing enough to reduce the problems in England's cities?
4. How does Stevenson appear to criticise the typical social attitudes shown in characters such as Mr Utterson and Dr Lanyon?

EXAM PRACTICE

This extract from Chapter 1 describes the side entrance to Dr Jekyll's house that is used by Mr Hyde.

'It was two storeys high; showed no window, nothing but a door on the lower storey and a blind forehead of discoloured wall on the upper; and bore in every feature, the marks of prolonged and sordid negligence. The door, which was equipped with neither bell nor knocker, was blistered and distained. Tramps slouched into the recess and struck matches on the panels; children kept shop upon the steps;'

Write a paragraph analysing how Stevenson presents some of England's social problems in the extract.

Victorian Values

You must be able to: understand the idea of Victorian values and how they appear in the novel.

What were Victorian values?

Wealthy Victorians – people living in the nineteenth century, under the reign of Queen Victoria – had a strict code of moral and social conduct. This meant that they had rigid beliefs and unwritten rules about how to live their lives, and these became stricter the higher people rose in society in terms of class and status. Nowadays, we refer to this code of conduct as Victorian values.

The reputation of a Victorian meant everything. It was vital to be well-respected and to be considered moral and worthy.

As part of this, appearance became of great importance. There were high expectations of behaviour, from the way people dressed and spoke, to the company they kept and how they ate their meals.

Regular attendance at church was expected and, linking to Christian values, moderation in all things (such as food or alcohol) was highly regarded.

The Victorians also believed in sexual restraint, with sex seen more as a way to create a family than as a source of pleasure. There was low tolerance of crime and the belief that criminals should be dealt with harshly.

Did the Victorians really live by these values?

Historians have noted the contrast between the Victorians' social values and the social problems that filled their cities.

Many middle class and upper class Victorians lived their life by this set of values. Some were happy to do so whilst others had to **repress** a desire not to.

However, plenty of Victorian gentlemen lived an almost double life. They appeared very moral and proper, and were seen in the right places doing the right things but would secretly indulge in vices such as prostitution, drunkenness, gambling and drug abuse. The more money they had, the better they could keep these vices hidden and maintain their reputation.

Stevenson himself is believed to have horrified his religious parents by visiting brothels and getting drunk.

How does Stevenson explore Victorian values?

Mr Utterson is typical of a good Victorian. He has a strict moral code, is charitable to others, is restrained in his enjoyments and worries about the reputation of his friends.

Dr Jekyll is the darker side of the Victorian era: a well-respected, professional man who hides a violent and corrupt nature. Stevenson suggests, through Jekyll's final confession, that all humankind has a dual nature that includes unpleasant characteristics.

Summary

- Victorian values were a strict moral and social code.
- Reputation was highly valued in Victorian society.
- The middle and upper classes expected each other to behave in a polite and respectable way, avoiding vice and living a life of restraint.
- Dr Jekyll is used by Stevenson to show that not all Victorians lived like this. For many, it was just a surface appearance, hiding immoral behaviour.

Questions

QUICK TEST
1. What things did Victorian values include?
2. Which character in the novel can be seen as representing particularly strong Victorian values?
3. In what way does Dr Jekyll display Victorian values?
4. In what way does Dr Jekyll represent a lack of Victorian values?

EXAM PRACTICE
This extract from Chapter 1 describes Mr Utterson's behaviour.

'At friendly meetings, and when the wine was to his taste, something eminently human beaconed from his eye; something indeed which never found its way into his talk, but which spoke not only in these silent symbols of the after-dinner face, but more often and loudly in the acts of his life. He was austere with himself; drank gin when he was alone, to mortify a taste for vintages; and though he enjoyed the theatre, had not crossed the doors of one for twenty years.'

Write a paragraph analysing how Stevenson presents Mr Utterson as typifying Victorian values in this extract.

Science, Evolution and Physiognomy

You must be able to: understand how Stevenson makes use of different scientific advances and theories in his novel.

What scientific developments influenced Stevenson's writing?

The nineteenth century saw many advances in chemistry and biology. Scientists such as Louis Pasteur and Robert Bunsen made important discoveries, new chemicals were identified and the first modern periodic table was published in 1869.

Stevenson refers to modern science in Dr Jekyll's experiments. By basing it on new scientific discoveries that people had heard of but didn't fully understand, the transformation of Jekyll into Hyde seems more realistic and, therefore, more frightening.

How is the theory of evolution linked to the novel?

Charles Darwin's theory of **evolution** was explained in his 1859 book, *On The Origin Of Species*, based on his studies during a five-year voyage around the world.

Darwin's book caused great controversy at the time because it conflicted with the teachings of the Church, suggesting that man evolved from apes.

Although Stevenson does not make any direct references to it, Dr Jekyll can be seen as an effect of Darwinism. He questions established ideas about humanity and the natural world, and wishes to tamper with what was previously seen as God's creation.

Stevenson also draws on evolution when describing Mr Hyde. When Poole, for example, refers to him as 'a masked thing like a monkey' in Chapter 8, Stevenson uses Darwinism to create a sense of de-evolution (the reverse of evolution) as if Mr Hyde is a lower form of human life.

How is physiognomy linked to Mr Hyde?

Stevenson also makes use of the more popular, and completely unscientific, belief in physiognomy. This **pseudoscience** asserted that a person's character and personality could be assessed from their outward appearance, particularly the face. This links with the importance of appearance in Victorian society.

One of the ways in which the reader and the other characters know that Mr Hyde is evil is because he 'looks' evil. The novel is full of descriptions of Hyde's strange facial appearance, his shrunken body and his strange way of walking. In Chapter 1, Enfield describes him as having, 'something wrong with his appearance, something displeasing; something downright detestable'. Hyde's appearance is presented using a **pattern of three** negative **verbs** to show he is a bad person. This is emphasised by the **repetition** of the **pronoun** 'something' to create mystery and capture Enfield's feelings of unease.

Rather than promoting physiognomy, Stevenson is using it to play on – and criticise – his readers' social prejudices. He deliberately makes Jekyll 'look' comparatively good so the twist of the novel is unexpected.

Summary

- The nineteenth century saw many advances in chemistry. Stevenson draws on this to make Jekyll's transformation into Hyde seem more realistic.
- Stevenson also makes use of Darwinism in his characterisation of Jekyll and the way in which Hyde is described.
- Descriptions of Jekyll and Hyde also link to the popular pseudoscience of physiognomy in order to play on the readers' expectations.

Questions

QUICK TEST
1. Why might Stevenson want Jekyll's transformation into Hyde to seem like a realistic possibility?
2. How are descriptions of Hyde linked to ideas of evolution?
3. What was physiognomy?
4. How is physiognomy used to present Hyde as evil?

EXAM PRACTICE
This extract from Chapter 9 features Dr Lanyon's description of Mr Hyde.

'... there was something abnormal and misbegotten in the very essence of the creature that now faced me – something seizing, surprising, and revolting – this fresh disparity seemed but to fit in with and to reinforce it; so that to my interest in the man's nature and character, there was added a curiosity as to his origin, his life, his fortune and status in the world.'

Write a paragraph analysing how Stevenson uses Victorian interests in evolution and/or physiognomy to present Mr Hyde in this extract.

Gothic Horror

You must be able to: understand how the novel uses different features of genre.

What is Gothic horror?

Gothic horror is a genre of fiction that became popular in the late 1700s. Novels such as *The Castle of Otranto* and *Frankenstein* introduced readers to the enjoyment of being scared.

The key elements of this genre are frightening events, supernatural occurrences, sinister old settings like castles, mystery, doubles and disguise, and romance.

How does the novel fit into the genre of Gothic horror?

Although Gothic horror was never critically acclaimed, it was a popular genre with readers. In the late 1800s, writers modernised the genre to fit it into **contemporary** urban settings.

Stevenson's 1886 novel has sinister settings but they are the streets and buildings of nineteenth-century London. Similarly, the strange and frightening events are linked to modern science rather than to the supernatural.

Stevenson focusses on the mystery and how the theme of doubles could explore modern Victorian identity and attitudes. Instead of romance, there is a sense of tragedy at what Jekyll does to himself.

Does the novel fit into any other genres?

There are aspects of detective fiction in the novel. This was also a popular genre in the late 1800s and the first Sherlock Holmes stories appeared the year after *Dr Jekyll and Mr Hyde* was published.

Mr Utterson sets forth to solve the mystery of Mr Hyde; there is a murder case, different clues and evidence to be pieced together, the possibility of blackmail and he even works alongside the police in Chapter 4.

In addition, through the fantastical exploration of scientific advances, the novel can be seen as using elements of the science fiction genre that had begun to gain popularity in the nineteenth century.

Stevenson's novel can also be placed in a genre known as *fin de siècle*, which means 'end of the century' in French. This was an idea that, as the new century loomed, society had become **decadent** and **degenerate**. A series of nineteenth-century novels explored this idea, incorporating themes of evolution, corruption and anxiety about the state of humanity.

Summary

- The novel was a modern version of the Gothic genre, describing strange events in a contemporary nineteenth-century setting.
- It also features elements of other genres, such as detective and science fiction.
- Stevenson uses popular forms of literature while exploring complex ideas about human behaviour.
- The negative view of humanity that is created through the character of Mr Hyde also places the novel in the genre known as *fin de siècle*.

Questions

QUICK TEST

1. What aspects of Gothic horror feature in the novel?
2. How were these genre features modernised by Stevenson to match his nineteenth-century audience?
3. What features of detective fiction and science fiction also appear in the novel?
4. What anxieties about the modern world does Stevenson explore in the novel?

EXAM PRACTICE

This extract from Chapter 4 describes the involvement of Mr Utterson in the investigation of Sir Danvers Carew's murder.

'Mr Utterson had already quailed at the name of Hyde; but when the stick was laid before him, he could doubt no longer; broken and battered as it was, he recognised it for one that he had himself presented many years before to Henry Jekyll.

Mr. Utterson reflected; and then, raising his head, "If you will come with me in my cab," he said, "I think I can take you to his house."

It was by this time about nine in the morning, and the first fog of the season. A great chocolate-coloured **pall** lowered over heaven, but the wind was continually charging and routing these embattled vapours; so that as the cab crawled from street to street, Mr. Utterson beheld a marvellous number of degrees and hues of twilight; for here it would be dark like the back-end of evening; and there would be a glow of a rich, lurid brown, like the light of some strange conflagration; and here, for a moment, the fog would be quite broken up, and a haggard shaft of daylight would glance in between the swirling wreaths.'

Write a paragraph analysing how Stevenson uses different genre features in the extract to engage his readers.

Dr Jekyll's Setting

You must be able to: analyse the significance of Dr Jekyll's setting.

What is significant about the exterior of Dr Jekyll's home?

Stevenson uses Dr Jekyll's house to suggest things about the character.

In Chapter 2, Jekyll's home is described using the **adjectives** 'ancient, handsome' to suggest reliability and respectability. It also has 'a great air of wealth and comfort' and these **abstract nouns** reflect Dr Jekyll's profession and social status.

The way the house looks links to the importance of appearance in Victorian society. Because this is the front of the house, it also reminds the reader how good appearances can sometimes be superficial.

What is significant about the interior of the house?

The reader is told, in Chapter 2, that the hallway has 'a bright, open fire and furnished with costly cabinets of oak'. Adjectives such as 'bright' and 'open' suggest goodness, honesty and friendliness, while 'costly' implies wealth and status.

However, when Mr Utterson notices 'a menace in the flickering of the firelight [...] the shadow on the roof', Stevenson is using **foreshadowing** to suggest that something nasty is hiding beneath the nice surface.

This continues in Chapter 5 when the reader is told about Dr Jekyll's laboratory. The adjectives 'dingy, windowless' imply corruption and secrecy, while the description of it 'lying gaunt and silent' creates a sinister atmosphere. Stevenson also makes the door to Dr Jekyll's private room (the 'cabinet') red, as if to **symbolise** danger.

What is significant about the area in which Dr Jekyll lives?

In Chapter 1, Stevenson describes the area in which Dr Jekyll lives as being clean, tidy, and well-kept, symbolising respectability. The inhabitants are 'emulously hoping to do better', with the **adverb** suggesting that they all follow, good middle class values in order to keep improving their lives.

The attractiveness of the shop fronts is conveyed using the **simile**, 'like smiling saleswomen', but this could also be interpreted as linking to superficiality (trying to 'sell' an appearance of respectability).

There are suggestions that Dr Jekyll is encircled by corruption. The local shops are contrasted with the 'dingy' surrounding neighbourhood while, in Chapter 2, the houses on either side of Dr Jekyll's are 'decayed from their high estate' and sometimes rented out to 'shady lawyers'. This could present Dr Jekyll as a figure of superiority, it could link to the way in which he is tempted by immorality or it could emphasise how he keeps his own lack of **propriety** hidden.

Summary

- Stevenson uses the setting to suggest things about Dr Jekyll.
- The good appearance of the house and the area in which he lives suggest that he is a good person.
- However, different references to darkness, shadows and corruption are used to imply another side to his character.
- These descriptions of the setting link to the importance of appearance and status in Victorian society, and the way in which this sometimes hid a less moral reality.

Questions

QUICK TEST
1. How is the area in which Dr Jekyll lives made to sound respectable?
2. What features of Dr Jekyll's home sound pleasant and welcoming?
3. How does Dr Jekyll's home reflect his social status?
4. What is the least welcoming part of Dr Jekyll's home?

EXAM PRACTICE
This extract from Chapter 1 describes the local area in which Dr Jekyll lives.

'Even on Sunday, when it veiled its more florid charms and lay comparatively empty of passage, the street shone out in contrast to its dingy neighbourhood, like a fire in a forest; and with its freshly painted shutters, well-polished brasses, and general cleanliness and gaiety of note, instantly caught and pleased the eye of the passenger.'

Write a paragraph analysing how Stevenson uses settings to suggest things about the character of Dr Jekyll.

Mr Hyde's Setting

You must be able to: analyse the significance of Mr Hyde's setting.

What is significant about Mr Hyde's entrance to Dr Jekyll's house?

In Chapter 1, Mr Hyde uses a back entrance to Dr Jekyll's house. Stevenson uses negative images to contrast this entrance with the pretty local shops and the later descriptions of Dr Jekyll's house in Chapter 2.

As well as creating mystery for the reader, the contrasts symbolise how Mr Hyde represents the dark, **sinful** side of Dr Jekyll's character.

This section of the house is described as 'sinister' and **personification** in 'thrust forward its gable' makes it sound aggressive and unfriendly. The fact it is windowless suggests secrecy, the descriptions of neglect and 'tramps slouched into the recess' shows a lack of respectability and the door itself looks almost diseased to imply corruption and immorality.

What is significant about the area in which Mr Hyde lives?

Mr Hyde lives in Soho and this is used to establish his immoral character. When the novel was written, in 1886, Soho had a bad reputation as one of London's most over-populated and run-down areas, suffering several cholera outbreaks in the 1850s.

Many immigrants had settled in the area (against whom the Victorians were often prejudiced) and there was much poverty. In the novel, Stevenson refers to 'women of many different nationalities' and 'ragged children'.

Prostitution had become a thriving trade so Stevenson mentions the 'slatternly' locals. There were many disreputable pubs and music halls in Soho and Mr Utterson disparagingly notices the 'gin palace'.

In Chapter 4, Stevenson creates sinister descriptions of the area. There are 'swirling wreaths' of fog (with the **noun** 'wreath' linking to death), the streets are 'muddy' and 'dingy', and a simile is used to show how Mr Utterson sees it as 'like a district of some city in a nightmare'.

Stevenson also links Soho to Hell to suggest immorality. Describing the fog as 'a great chocolate-coloured pall lowered over heaven' uses **metaphor** to imply unholiness and create another link to death. Simile is used for a similar purpose with 'like the light of some strange conflagration' suggesting the fires of Hell and damnation.

What is significant about the interior of his lodgings?

To develop mystery and begin to establish the idea that Mr Hyde *is* Dr Jekyll, Stevenson makes the rooms that he rents uncharacteristically 'furnished with luxury and good taste'.

Stevenson lists the fine wines, good artwork and pleasant decor to build up a contrast with the Soho streets outside. Again, setting is being used to explore identity, appearance and respectability.

Summary

- Stevenson uses the setting to suggest things about Mr Hyde.
- The neglected back entrance to Dr Jekyll's house suggests that he is an immoral and corrupt person.
- This is emphasised by the descriptions of Soho, which was infamous for vice, poverty and disease in the nineteenth century.
- However, the contrasting interior luxury of his lodgings creates mystery and links to how Dr Jekyll is the better side of Mr Hyde's identity.

Questions

QUICK TEST
1. In Chapters 1 and 2, what are the descriptions of Mr Hyde's door meant to be contrasted with by the reader?
2. Why was Soho seen as a bad area in the nineteenth century?
3. What does Stevenson link Soho to in order to suggest it is corrupt and unholy?
4. How are Mr Hyde's lodgings linked to Dr Jekyll's character rather than Mr Hyde's?

EXAM PRACTICE
This extract from Chapter 1 describes Mr Hyde's side entrance into Dr Jekyll's house.

'... a certain sinister block of building thrust forward its gable on the street. It was two storeys high; showed no window, nothing but a door on the lower storey and a blind forehead of discoloured wall on the upper; and bore in every feature, the marks of prolonged and sordid negligence. The door, which was equipped with neither bell nor knocker, was blistered and distained.'

Write a paragraph analysing how Stevenson uses settings to suggest things about the character of Mr Hyde.

You must be able to: analyse how Stevenson establishes the character of Dr Jekyll.

How is Dr Jekyll presented as a respectable Victorian gentleman?

In the first eight chapters, Stevenson withholds the truth and presents Dr Jekyll as a fairly typical Victorian gentleman.

His title suggests a sensible, professional man, and his home implies wealth and respectability. At the start of Chapter 3, different adjectives show his goodness by describing his 'pleasant dinners' and the company he keeps as 'all intelligent, reputable men'.

Dr Jekyll has an honest, friendly appearance: 'a large, well-made, smooth-faced man of fifty' who displays 'every mark of capacity and kindness'.

How does Stevenson establish mystery about Dr Jekyll?

The reader does not find out that Mr Hyde is Dr Jekyll's violent **alter ego** until the final two chapters. Instead, he is presented as Mr Hyde's victim. Strange clues create mystery and the reader is encouraged to wonder why he would associate with someone like Mr Hyde.

Dr Jekyll speaks **ambiguously** of him, saying 'I do sincerely take a great, a very great interest in that young man' but also 'The moment I choose, I can be rid of Mr Hyde'. After Sir Danvers Carew's murder, he claims Mr Hyde has gone away but adds, 'I have grounds for certainty that I cannot share with anyone'.

Dr Jekyll's will implies that he expects his own 'disappearance or unexplained absence'. Mr Utterson considers Dr Jekyll's 'wild' past and suspects his friend is being blackmailed, using the metaphors 'the ghost of some old sin, the cancer of some concealed disgrace'. Later, he fears that Dr Jekyll has forged a letter to aid Mr Hyde's escape.

His disagreement with Dr Lanyon – and therefore the true nature of his experiments – is kept vague. Dr Lanyon only refers to 'unscientific balderdash', and his criticism of 'scientific heresies' is repeated by an annoyed Dr Jekyll. This mystery increases when Dr Lanyon sends Mr Utterson a document that is not to be read until Dr Jekyll's 'death or disappearance'.

How is Dr Jekyll presented as troubled?

Dr Jekyll's behaviour becomes increasingly erratic and suspicious. He is clearly disturbed when Mr Utterson raises the subject of Mr Hyde in Chapter 3, and is later described as 'feverish' when he hears about Mr Hyde killing Sir Danvers Carew.

His self-imposed isolation in Chapter 6 suggests something is wrong, as does his sudden 'expression of such abject terror and despair' in the next chapter. When he vanishes in Chapter 8, it is presumed by Mr Utterson and Poole that he has been murdered by Mr Hyde.

Key Quotations to Learn

The large handsome face of Dr Jekyll grew pale to the very lips, and there came a blackness about his eyes. (Chapter 3)

'Utterson, I swear to God,' cried the doctor. 'I swear to God I will never set eyes on him again.' (Chapter 5)

... taking the air with an infinite sadness of **mien**, like some disconsolate prisoner ... (Chapter 7)

Summary

- Dr Jekyll is initially presented as a Victorian gentleman, with the truth about Mr Hyde held back until the last two chapters.
- Stevenson creates mystery through Dr Jekyll's association with someone who seems the opposite of his character.
- He is ambiguous when discussing Mr Hyde and there are different suggestions that he is being blackmailed or manipulated.
- Dr Jekyll's behaviour becomes increasingly strange and isolating during the novel.

Sample Analysis

Stevenson creates mystery around Dr Jekyll when he discusses his will with Mr Utterson, 'I am painfully situated, Utterson; my position is a very strange – a very strange one'. The adverb 'painfully' shows something is wrong but this is kept ambiguous through Stevenson's withholding of information and the use of the adjective 'strange'. This is emphasised through its repetition and the pause created by the dash to suggest Dr Jekyll's speech is anxious and evasive. By using words that link to status ('situated' and 'position'), the audience are reminded of the importance of reputation in Victorian society and led to consider whether the doctor has been compromised in some way.

Questions

QUICK TEST
1. How does Dr Jekyll's title link to his character?
2. What is significant about Dr Jekyll's personal appearance?
3. What hint is the reader given about Dr Jekyll's past?
4. In what way do Mr Utterson's fears about Dr Jekyll increase during the novel?

EXAM PRACTICE
Using one or more of the 'Key Quotations to Learn', write a paragraph analysing how Stevenson establishes the character of Dr Jekyll.

Dr Jekyll's Development

You must be able to: analyse how Stevenson develops the character of Dr Jekyll.

How does Dr Lanyon's narrative develop the reader's understanding of Dr Jekyll?

Chapter 9 develops the image of Dr Jekyll as a mad scientist. After reading his letter, Dr Lanyon believes his old friend to be 'insane' and suffering from 'cerebral disease'.

When Dr Lanyon collects Dr Jekyll's chemicals, Stevenson includes lots of scientific language (such as phial, phosphorus and ether) alongside dramatic adjectives (for example, blood-red and volatile) to suggest strange and dangerous experiments.

The end of the chapter features Stevenson's narrative reveal, with Mr Hyde transforming back into Dr Jekyll.

Dr Lanyon refers to Dr Jekyll's 'moral turpitude' and his 'tears of penitence', reminding the reader of the murder of Sir Danvers Carew, and describes how his own 'soul sickened'. This presents Dr Jekyll not as the Victorian gentleman previously established but as a disturbed man full of sin and regret.

How does the final chapter explain Dr Jekyll's character?

Stevenson makes the final chapter a first-person narrative written by Dr Jekyll in order to explain the mysteries that he has established and to develop his exploration of Victorian society.

Jekyll is presented as a man with conflicting desires: the wish to be respected ('carry my head high') and the wish to enjoy himself ('a certain impatient gaiety of disposition'). This conflict leads him to hide one half of his nature: 'I concealed my pleasures' and 'hid them with an almost morbid sense of shame'. The contrasting abstract nouns (pleasures/shame) emphasise his internal conflict while the verbs show his repression.

Dr Jekyll begins to explore the 'primitive duality of man' and Stevenson does this to comment on what he saw as the **duplicitous** and **hypocritical** nature of Victorian society. Because of censorship at the time the novel was written, and in order to create more mystery, Stevenson is vague about Dr Jekyll specific pleasures but the novel contains subtle references to alcohol, violence, drug abuse and sex with prostitutes.

Metaphor is used to show the happy feelings of freedom that he gains from transforming into Mr Hyde: 'shook the doors of the prison house of my disposition' and 'spring headlong into a sea of liberty'.

He is 'aghast' at what he is capable of, using metaphor to describe being 'plunged into a kind of wonder at my vicarious depravity'. However, although he feels **guilt**, he continually disassociates himself from this behaviour by attributing it to Mr Hyde.

Key Quotations to Learn

I have been doomed to such a shipwreck: that man is not truly one, but truly two.*
I was conscious of no repugnance, rather a leap of welcome. This, too, was myself.*
I stood already committed to a profound duplicity of me.*   (*Dr Jekyll: Chapter 10)

Summary

- Dr Lanyon's narrative presents Dr Jekyll as a mad, sinful scientist.
- Dr Jekyll's own narrative reveals his dual nature: a wish to be respected and a wish to indulge in dubious pleasures.
- Dr Jekyll feels free as Mr Hyde but is also shocked by his behaviour.
- Stevenson uses this development of Dr Jekyll's character to comment on how Victorian society is repressed and hypocritical.

Sample Analysis

Dr Jekyll's first-person narrative states that, 'it was the curse of mankind that these incongruous faggots be thus bound together', revealing frustration with his own sense of duality. The adjective 'incongruous' shows Dr Jekyll's belief that everyone has two conflicting sides to their personality, whilst the verb 'bound' implies that these opposites create personal restrictions, linking to Stevenson's criticism of Victorian repression. The **noun phrase**, 'curse of mankind' suggests that Dr Jekyll blames God for this situation, a **blasphemous** idea in the Christian society of the nineteenth century. This explains the motivation for his experiments (which he reveals Lanyon considered 'heresies') as well as implying that he may see himself as **damned**: 'faggots' is used as a metaphor for the self but means firewood so could be linked to burning in Hell.

Questions

QUICK TEST
1. What is the narrative revelation at the end of Chapter 9?
2. What conclusion does Dr Lanyon make about Dr Jekyll after reading his letter and visiting his laboratory?
3. What does Dr Jekyll say he spent most of his life doing about the things that he takes pleasure in?
4. Why doesn't Stevenson make it clear exactly what Dr Jekyll's sinful pleasures are?

EXAM PRACTICE
Using one or more of the 'Key Quotations to Learn', write a paragraph analysing how Stevenson develops the character of Dr Jekyll later in the novel.

Mr Hyde

You must be able to: analyse how Stevenson presents the character of Mr Hyde.

What does Stevenson use Mr Hyde to represent?

As the **homophone** suggests, Mr Hyde represents the dark side of human nature that people hide away. In particular, Stevenson uses him to reveal the reality behind the veneer of Victorian respectability.

Stevenson does not celebrate the bad parts of our identity but he asserts that not admitting they exist is untruthful and hypocritical.

What is significant about Mr Hyde's appearance?

Using the popular pseudoscience of physiognomy, Stevenson makes Mr Hyde look small, pale and unusual, implying that he is morally inferior.

Descriptions often focus on how Mr Hyde makes others feel rather than on specifically how he looks. Dr Lanyon describes 'something seizing, surprising, and revolting', using a pattern of three adjectives to convey his own negative reaction while the **sibilance** and the ambiguity in 'something' suggest – but do not pinpoint – how sinister Mr Hyde seems.

He is described as having 'a strong feeling of deformity', despite not actually being deformed. This is to suggest that Mr Hyde's true monstrosity is on the inside and, in Chapter 2, Mr Utterson reflects on this through the metaphor of the 'radiance of a foul soul'.

Drawing on Darwin's theory of evolution, Stevenson presents Mr Hyde as subhuman through simian references such as the simile, 'masked thing like a monkey'. He also links him to Hell, with Mr Utterson metaphorically seeing 'Satan's signature' on his face.

In Chapter 10, Stevenson describes Mr Hyde's hand as 'dusky' and 'swarthy', drawing on the typical Victorian prejudice against foreignness to suggest degeneracy.

How does Mr Hyde behave?

Mr Hyde is described as having 'a black sneering coolness'; this phrase uses **traditional** colour symbolism to present him as evil whilst also implying a sense of status and superiority (to hint at his true identity as a wealthy and respectable Victorian gentleman).

Mr Hyde diverges from expected Victorian behaviour through his sometimes uncontrolled speech. For example, '"He never told you", cried Mr Hyde with a flush of anger' and '"Have you got it?" he cried. "Have you got it?"'.

He is aggressive and is depicted using powerful verbs, such as 'snarled aloud into a savage laugh' and 'clubbed him to the earth'. The words 'savage' and 'clubbed' also suggest de-evolution by linking to Stone Age man.

The killing of Sir Danvers shows Hyde at his most violent; the metaphor 'a storm of blows, under which the bones were audibly shattered' captures his uncontrollable rage.

Key Quotations to Learn

'It wasn't like a man; it was like some damned juggernaut.' (Mr Enfield: Chapter 1)

… with apelike fury, he was trampling his victim underfoot … (Chapter 4)

… something abnormal and misbegotten in the very essence of the creature …
(Dr Lanyon: Chapter 9)

Summary

- Stevenson uses the pseudoscience of physiognomy to show that Mr Hyde is evil.
- He is often described through the negative reactions he provokes in others.
- He is violent and uncontrollable.
- Stevenson draws on Darwin's ideas of evolution to present Mr Hyde as subhuman.

Sample Analysis

Mr Hyde is described as 'pale and dwarfish, he gave an impression of deformity without any nameable malformation', with Stevenson using the popular pseudoscience of physiognomy to make him seem instantly evil. The idea that his 'deformity' cannot actually be seen implies that it is an internal, moral 'malformation'. The reference to his pallor also suggests that he is in some way diseased, while his small stature is used to symbolise his lack of social status and accompanying values. Descriptions like this help to elicit the reader's surprise and highlight Stevenson's idea that evil lies in all of us when Mr Hyde is later revealed to be Dr Jekyll.

Questions

QUICK TEST
1. How is Mr Hyde's surname relevant?
2. Which animal is Mr Hyde linked to and what is the significance of this?
3. How is Mr Hyde linked to Hell?
4. Is Mr Hyde's true evil on the outside or the inside?

EXAM PRACTICE
Using one or more of the 'Key Quotations to Learn', write a paragraph analysing how Stevenson presents the character of Mr Hyde.

Jekyll and Hyde's Struggle for Dominance

You must be able to: analyse how Stevenson conveys the battle for control between Jekyll and Hyde.

How do Dr Jekyll's feelings about Mr Hyde begin to change?

In Chapter 10, Stevenson uses a pattern of three comparative adjectives to show Dr Jekyll's pleasure at first transforming into Mr Hyde: 'I felt younger, lighter, happier'. His new body is 'less robust and less developed than the good which I had just deposed', suggesting his good side has always dominated. The verb 'deposed' suggests he has cast off his moral side as well as foreshadowing the later fight for control.

He describes his pleasures becoming more immoral, 'they soon began to turn towards the monstrous', suggesting increasing self-disgust.

How does Stevenson show Mr Hyde getting stronger?

Dr Jekyll's first-person narrative refers to 'Edward Hyde' in the third person to suggest he is a separate entity. He also refers a few times to 'Henry Jekyll' to show their separation but, by the end of Chapter 10, he does this much more (regularly using the pronoun 'he' instead of 'I' when referring to Jekyll) to show Hyde's dominance.

When Jekyll involuntarily transforms into Mr Hyde, he reasons that his evil side has 'been much exercised and nourished', using verbs to suggest greater strength.

After resisting Hyde for two months, Jekyll gives in to temptation. Stevenson uses the metaphor, 'My devil had been long caged, he came out roaring', to convey Hyde's increased strength, and emphasises this by repeating similar images of damnation and anger.

The transformations become more involuntary, each time being more difficult to change back. By the end of Chapter 10, 'The powers of Hyde seemed to have grown with the sickliness of Jekyll', and Stevenson describes, 'The hatred of Hyde for Jekyll'.

It becomes less of a battle between the two, more of a continual persecution by Hyde, 'scrawling in my own hand blasphemies on the pages of my books, burning the letters, and destroying the portrait of my father', presenting an assault on Jekyll's identity and values that are summarised as Hyde's 'apelike spite'.

How does Stevenson make the transformation frightening?

The transformation in Chapter 9 is described as painful and violent to mirror the battle taking place between the two sides of Dr Jekyll's identity.

The pattern of three verbs, 'reeled, staggered, clutched' suggest pain, and the simile 'groping before him with his hands, like a man restored from death' implies that the transformation is a fight for survival.

Traditional colour symbolism is also used in 'his face became suddenly black' to create a nightmarish image that links to sin.

Key Quotations to Learn

The most racking pains succeeded: a grinding in the bones, deadly nausea, and a horror of the spirit ... (Dr Jekyll: Chapter 10)

... my new power tempted me until I fell into slavery. (Dr Jekyll: Chapter 10)

Instantly, the spirit of Hell awoke in me and raged. (Dr Jekyll: Chapter 10)

Summary

- Although Dr Jekyll initially welcomes the freedom and pleasures that Mr Hyde offers, he becomes increasingly horrified by Hyde's actions.
- The Mr Hyde side of Jekyll's personality becomes stronger and the transformations take place involuntarily.
- Stevenson gradually increases the way Jekyll refers to himself in the third person to show his struggle to control his dual identities and the dominance of Hyde.
- As Hyde takes control, he hates and persecutes the weaker Jekyll.

Sample Analysis

Stevenson shows Dr Jekyll's conflict with the darker side of his identity when he says of Mr Hyde: 'He, I say – I cannot say, I. That child of Hell had nothing human'. The repetition of the first-person pronoun displays his wish to assert his separation from Hyde but the proximity of the third-person pronoun, along with the pauses created by the dash and the commas, also suggest his confusion and the difficulty of separation. Similarly, the metaphor uses Christianity to link to traditional social values and express his difference to Hyde; however, the noun 'child' is included to remind the reader that Jekyll created Hyde and he comes from inside him (having compared the initial transformation to 'the hour of birth').

Questions

QUICK TEST
1. After first transforming, does Dr Jekyll feel better or worse in the body of Mr Hyde?
2. What reason is suggested for Mr Hyde's body being smaller than Dr Jekyll's body?
3. In what way is the Hyde personality different after being resisted for two months?
4. What events show that the Hyde personality has become stronger than Dr Jekyll?

EXAM PRACTICE
Using one or more of the 'Key Quotations to Learn', write a paragraph analysing how Stevenson presents the relationship between Jekyll and Hyde.

You must be able to: consider different ways in which readers might respond to Dr Jekyll.

How might readers view Dr Jekyll sympathetically?

Dr Jekyll is presented as a man with deeply conflicting attitudes. Hardworking and wishing to be respected, he also hides various unnamed, immoral pleasures and this leads to a feeling of shame. His experiments show a desire to understand humankind more, as well as a desperation to escape the 'seemingly so solid body in which we walk attired'.

Dr Jekyll is often shocked by Mr Hyde's behaviour. After changing back, he says he would 'even make haste, where it was possible, to undo the evil done by Hyde'.

After the murder of Sir Danvers Carew, Jekyll tries to 'redeem the past' and this verb indicates a religious attitude. Despite battling with his conscience, he cannot resist the life that Mr Hyde allows him and uses personification to describe how he 'fell before the assaults of temptation'.

He brings about his own downfall and eventually regrets his actions, using the metaphor 'sea of abhorrence' to show his self-disgust. His goodness can be seen in his attitude towards Mr Hyde, 'I find it in my heart to pity him'. Before he loses himself to Mr Hyde's control, he signs his 'confession', which emphasises the guilt he feels.

Why might Dr Jekyll be judged more harshly?

By his own admission, Dr Jekyll was born into a privileged life, with 'a large fortune' and 'every guarantee of an honourable and distinguished future'. As well as wanting people to look up to him and respect him publicly, he wants to be able to indulge in private vices and pleasures. This **dichotomy** shows the Christian sins of greed and pride (in addition to suggestions of lust and gluttony).

The creation of Mr Hyde allows Dr Jekyll to disassociate himself from the terrible crimes that he commits, including a physical assault on a child and the murder of an old gentleman.

He is warned about his experiments by his friend, Dr Lanyon, but ignores him ('that hidebound pedant Lanyon'). He is offered help by his friend, Mr Utterson ('Make a clean breast of this in confidence, and I make no doubt I can get you out of it'), but turns it down.

Even after he turns to Dr Lanyon for help, he still boasts about his experiments, 'you who have denied the virtue of transcendental medicine, you who have derided your superiors – behold!'

Key Quotations to Learn

Promising Utterson that he is never going to see Mr Hyde again: 'I bind my honour to you that I am done with him in this world. It is all at an end.' (Chapter 5)

Explaining his reclusion to Mr Utterson: 'I have brought on myself a punishment and a danger that I cannot name.' (Chapter 6)

Describing the murder of Sir Danvers: I mauled the unresisting body, tasting delight from every blow; (Chapter 10)

Summary

- It is possible to judge the character of Dr Jekyll in very different ways.
- Readers might sympathise with the things that led Dr Jekyll to create Mr Hyde and the way that this brought about his own destruction.
- Alternatively, readers might condemn his selfish behaviour and the crimes that he commits and blames on Mr Hyde.

Sample Analysis

Readers may have different responses towards Dr Jekyll. In Chapter 6, Stevenson uses **parallelism** in the phrase, 'If I am the chief of sinners, I am the chief of sufferers also', to present the contrasting ways in which the character might be judged. The reference to suffering elicits sympathy from the reader and we later discover the conflicting feelings that led Dr Jekyll to create Mr Hyde and his struggle for control. However, the reference to sin reminds the reader of his immorality and the crimes he has committed; a reader at the time the novel was published, when Victorian values were a dominant social factor and religion was a stronger part of everyday life, might be particularly inclined to condemn the character of Dr Jekyll. In addition, the use of the **conjunction** 'if' creates a negative view by implying either that he does not see himself as immoral or that he believes his difficulties excuse his actions.

Questions

QUICK TEST
1. What different feelings does Dr Jekyll display that might gain sympathy from a reader?
2. What crimes does Mr Hyde commit that make it easy to condemn Dr Jekyll?
3. Whose help and advice does Dr Jekyll ignore?

EXAM PRACTICE
Using one or more of the 'Key Quotations to Learn', write a paragraph presenting your own judgement of Dr Jekyll.

Mr Utterson

You must be able to: analyse how Stevenson presents the character of Mr Utterson.

What is Mr Utterson like and how is this shown?

Mr Utterson is a lawyer whose face is 'never lighted by a smile'. This miserable metaphor is developed through a list of negative adjectives, 'cold, scanty, and embarrassed in discourse; backward in sentiment; lean, long, dusty, dreary', presenting him as a quiet, reserved and serious man.

He is strict with himself; he avoids drinking too much wine, doesn't go to the theatre despite enjoying it and lives a sensible life. He is looked up to by others, with the police and Poole asking for his help, and even Dr Jekyll's cook 'crying out 'Bless God! It's Mr Utterson' in Chapter 8. This suggests a stereotypical Victorian gentleman.

Stevenson adds that Mr Utterson is 'somehow lovable' and that, perhaps unusually for a Victorian gentleman, he doesn't judge his friends: 'the last reputable acquaintance and the last good influence in the lives of downgoing men'.

What is Mr Utterson's relationship with Dr Jekyll?

Mr Utterson is one of Dr Jekyll's 'oldest friends'.

His worries about Dr Jekyll's relationship with Mr Hyde are shown through metaphor and simile: 'It turns me cold to think of this creature stealing like a thief to Harry's bedside'.

He tries to find out things about Mr Hyde that could be used to protect his friend, '"Hyde, if he were studied," thought he, "must have secrets of his own; black secrets by the look of him"'.

Although uncomfortable with the terms of Dr Jekyll's will, he looks after it and honourably accepts Dr Jekyll's wishes.

He helps to protect Dr Jekyll's respectability in Chapter 5 by taking charge of the letter from Mr Hyde. Metaphor is used to show his shock in realising that Dr Jekyll has forged the letter, 'his blood ran cold in his veins', but he does not report it to the police.

What role does Mr Utterson play in the narrative?

Stevenson uses Mr Utterson as the novel's protagonist. Although Dr Jekyll is the central character, it is Utterson's curiosity and his desire to help that develops the plot.

He is a semi-detective, investigating Mr Hyde, aiding the police, questioning evidence like the letter, piecing together clues (such as Lanyon's statement and Jekyll's final confession) and being in charge when Dr Jekyll's laboratory is broken into.

Narrated in the third person, Mr Utterson discovers things at the same pace as the reader, creating a relationship between the character and the reader.

Key Quotations to Learn

He was austere with himself; (Chapter 1)

'If he be Mr Hyde,' he thought, 'I shall be Mr Seek.' (Mr Utterson: Chapter 2)

'Ah, that's not Jekyll's voice – it's Hyde's!' cried Utterson. 'Down with the door, Poole!' (Chapter 8)

Summary

- Mr Utterson is described as a serious, restrained and professional man who wishes to help his friend, Dr Jekyll.

- In many ways, he is presented as a stereotypically honourable Victorian gentleman.

- However, he is willing to ignore a loss of respectability in his friends, conceals evidence from the police and has some past misdeeds of his own.

- He is the protagonist of the novel, in that Stevenson uses him to move the plot forward and reveal information to the reader.

Sample Analysis

Stevenson presents Mr Utterson as a flawed but generally good and honourable Victorian gentleman. Thinking about his past in Chapter 2, 'he was humbled to dust by the many ill things he had done and raised up again into a sober and fearful gratitude by the many he had come so near to doing yet avoided', the initial metaphor shows that Mr Utterson acknowledges his past sins and feels guilt. He appears to judge these crimes as being worse than they actually were. The verb 'humbled', along with the later noun phrase 'fearful gratitude', suggests feeling in the presence of a higher power, implying an adherence to the Christian values of the period. These lines – particularly through the verb 'avoided' – also show how he is restrained, suggesting a suppression of certain desires or wishes that makes him a contrast to Dr Jekyll.

Questions

QUICK TEST
1. How is Mr Utterson initially described by Stevenson in a negative way?
2. What are his positive characteristics?
3. In what ways does Mr Utterson keep his lifestyle controlled and moderate?
4. Why does he try to find out things about Mr Hyde?

EXAM PRACTICE
Using one or more of the 'Key Quotations to Learn', write a paragraph analysing how Stevenson presents the character of Mr Utterson and how he uses him in the novel.

Dr Lanyon

You must be able to: analyse how Stevenson presents the character of Dr Lanyon.

What is Dr Lanyon like and how is this shown?

In Chapter 2, Dr Lanyon is introduced through the adjective 'great' to show that he is a highly respected man. This is emphasised by the reference to his 'crowding patients' to imply that he is highly regarded in the medical world.

He is described using a list of adjectives, 'hearty, healthy, red-faced dapper gentleman' to establish him as lively and friendly.

When Dr Lanyon appears again, in Chapter 6, he is very different: 'The rosy man had grown pale; his flesh had fallen away; he was visibly balder and older'. He is also described as having a look of 'some deep-seated terror of the mind'.

What is Dr Lanyon's relationship with Dr Jekyll?

Like Mr Utterson, Dr Lanyon is an old friend of Dr Jekyll. However, in Chapter 2, he is described as 'flushing suddenly purple' in anger at the mention of Dr Jekyll's experiments. He describes them as 'such unscientific balderdash' but Stevenson withholds any further detail to build up the atmosphere of mystery.

His discomfort at the mention of Dr Jekyll's name is increased in Chapter 6, 'I wish to see or hear no more of Dr Jekyll […] whom I regard as dead'. Once more, Stevenson creates mystery by withholding the reasons for Dr Lanyon's sudden illness and his attitude towards Dr Jekyll until Chapter 9.

What role does Dr Lanyon play in the narrative?

As well as using his character to establish mystery in the early chapters, Stevenson writes Chapter 9 (featuring the dramatic transformation scene) from Dr Lanyon's perspective.

One of the reasons that Stevenson establishes Dr Lanyon as a reputable man of science is to make this account seem more reliable – and therefore scarier – to his readers. Similarly, the early references to his good heath emphasise his sickened reaction to Dr Jekyll's experiments.

When he witnesses the transformation, metaphor is used to describe Dr Lanyon's horror, 'my mind submerged in terror', and this is emphasised by the inclusion of exclamative speech: '"Oh God!" I screamed, and "Oh God!" again and again'. The repeated reference to God also implies the evil nature of Dr Jekyll's work.

In his narrative, Dr Lanyon says that he will not repeat what Dr Jekyll tells him of his experiments and that he cannot 'dwell on it without a start of horror'. Again, Stevenson is withholding information to keep the reader engaged.

Key Quotations to Learn

… he sprang up from his chair and welcomed him with both hands. (Chapter 2)

He had his death warrant written legibly upon his face. (Chapter 6)

I saw what I saw, I heard what I heard, and my soul sickened at it; (Dr Lanyon: Chapter 9)

Summary

- Dr Lanyon is presented as a sensible and respectable Victorian gentleman.
- Stevenson uses the character of Dr Lanyon to create mystery in the novel.
- He is introduced as a happy, healthy man but he has had a disagreement with Dr Jekyll; he later falls suddenly ill and refuses to talk about him.
- Dr Lanyon's perspective is used in Chapter 9 to make the transformation frightening.

Sample Analysis

Stevenson uses metaphor and personification to describe Dr Lanyon's shocked reaction to Dr Jekyll's experiments. His first-person perspective, 'My life is shaken to its roots; sleep has left me; the deadliest terror sits by me at all hours' creates an immediate and intimate response that increases the atmosphere of horror for the reader. This is particularly evident in the use of the **superlative** and the feeling that he is haunted by his experience, while the reference to loss of sleep emphasises the idea that Dr Jekyll's experiments are unnatural. The first clause shows how Dr Lanyon's values and beliefs have been unsettled and this could link to the way in which Stevenson is using his tale of Dr Jekyll to expose the reality and hypocrisy of Victorian society.

Questions

QUICK TEST

1. In Chapter 2, what is his opinion of Dr Jekyll's scientific experiments?
2. How does Dr Lanyon's appearance change, according to Chapter 6, after witnessing the transformation that he describes in Chapter 9?
3. What information related to Dr Lanyon does Stevenson withhold in order to create mystery?
4. How is establishing Dr Lanyon as a reliable, educated man meant to affect the reader's response to his narrative in Chapter 9?

EXAM PRACTICE

Using one or more of the 'Key Quotations to Learn', write a paragraph analysing how Stevenson presents the character of Dr Lanyon and how he uses him in the novel.

Mr Enfield and Poole

You must be able to: analyse how Stevenson presents the characters of Mr Enfield and Poole.

What are Mr Enfield and Poole like and how is this shown?

Mr Richard Enfield and Poole are from opposite ends of the social spectrum. The former is 'the well-known man about town', suggesting he is wealthy and fashionable, while Poole is 'a well-dressed elderly servant' for Dr Jekyll.

Despite their differences, the men display shared values. Both are polite, addressing Mr Utterson as 'Sir' (although Poole is expected to use this form of address because Mr Utterson is his social superior). Both are discrete, with Enfield not enquiring too much about Mr Hyde because he has 'delicacy' and Poole turning to Mr Utterson, rather than the police, when he fears something has happened to Dr Jekyll. The two men are also loosely linked to Christianity, through Poole's phrase 'I give you my Bible word' and the various comparisons that Mr Enfield draws between Mr Hyde and Hell.

What role does Mr Enfield play in the narrative?

Mr Enfield provides the reader with their first impression of Mr Hyde, relating the incident with the young girl. He admits to an instant 'loathing' of Mr Hyde and describes a similar reaction from the girl's family and the doctor.

Through Mr Enfield's suspicions, Stevenson provides the reader with hints of mystery: Mr Hyde's strange appearance, his violent behaviour, his ability to get someone to write him a cheque for a lot of money and the suggestion of blackmail.

What role does Poole play in the narrative?

Poole's appearance at Mr Utterson's house is used to create narrative tension in Chapter 8.

He looks different, is frightened and talks evasively, '"I've been afraid for about a week," returned Poole, doggedly disregarding the question, "and I can bear it no more."'

To show Poole's anxiety and also to suggest the veneer of Victorian respectability, Stevenson describes the servant losing his temper: '"Hold your tongue!" Poole said to her with a ferocity of accent that testified to his own jangled nerves'.

The character of Poole is also used to create mystery. He describes Dr Jekyll's recent strange behaviour and introduces the idea that Mr Hyde is pretending to be the doctor, 'Have I been twenty years in this man's house, to be deceived by his voice?'

Poole's descriptions also create a disturbing image of Mr Hyde pacing back and forth inside the cabinet and once 'Weeping like a woman or a lost soul'.

Key Quotations to Learn

Mr Enfield about Mr Hyde: '... gave me one look so ugly that it brought out the sweat on me like running.' (Chapter 1)

About Poole: ... his face was white and his voice, when he spoke, was harsh and broken. (Chapter 8)

Poole about Mr Hyde: '... it went down my spine like ice.' (Chapter 8)

Summary

- Mr Enfield and Poole are socially very different but display similar Victorian values.
- Both characters are used to build up horror and mystery about Mr Hyde.
- The change in Poole's appearance and behaviour helps to create tension in Chapter 8 by showing that something is seriously wrong.

Sample Analysis

Stevenson uses the character of Poole to create mystery and horror in chapter 8. He suspects that someone is masquerading as Dr Jekyll, '"Sir," said the butler, turning to a sort of mottled pallor, "that thing was not my master"', with the vague noun 'thing' suggesting it is inhuman. This is emphasised by the contrast with the more respectful noun 'master' and obscures exactly what it is Poole has seen; the reader begins to guess but does not know that it is Hyde. The phrase that describes Poole's pale face also helps to build up a frightening atmosphere by showing how the mere memory of what he has seen sickens Poole.

Questions

QUICK TEST
1. In what way are Mr Enfield and Poole social opposites?
2. What similar values do the two men display?
3. What feelings does Mr Enfield display towards Mr Hyde?
4. What emotions does Poole display in Chapter 8?

EXAM PRACTICE
Using one or more of the 'Key Quotations to Learn', write a paragraph analysing how Stevenson uses the character of Poole or Mr Enfield to present Mr Hyde.

Good and Evil

You must be able to: analyse how Stevenson explores the themes of good and evil.

How is evil explored in the novel?

Stevenson uses Mr Hyde to represent evil and this is shown through the way the character looks, behaves and speaks.

Stevenson uses the pseudoscience of physiognomy to suggest that Mr Hyde's evil can be seen on his face, 'the man seems hardly human! Something **troglodytic'**.

He describes Mr Hyde's violent actions, such as the contrasting verb and adverb in 'trampled calmly' to show Mr Hyde's disregard for the girl's injuries in Chapter 1.

In Chapter 10, he uses powerful language to convey Mr Hyde's evil impulses, 'shaken with inordinate anger, strung to the pitch of murder, lusting to inflict pain'.

His viciousness and inhumanity are also captured through the way he speaks, 'snarled aloud into a savage laugh'. Stevenson emphasises Mr Hyde's otherness. In addition, Stevenson links Mr Hyde to evil through biblical language such as 'Satan', 'damned' and 'Hell'.

How is goodness explored in the novel?

Dr Jekyll is the good to Mr Hyde's evil. He has a respectable appearance and the metaphor 'good shone upon the countenance' implies his virtuous nature. Similarly, in Chapter 6, Stevenson adds that, 'he had always been known for charities, he was now no less distinguished for religion'.

Mr Utterson and Dr Lanyon are also presented as good men and this can be extended to minor characters such as Poole and Mr Enfield. Although none are perfect, they all display respectable behaviour, acts of kindness and Christian values.

How does Stevenson explore the conflict between good and evil?

In the nineteenth century, human nature was often presented as being either good or evil. Stevenson felt this was too simplistic and **disingenuous**. Through the character of Dr Jekyll, he presents humankind as containing both good and evil, acknowledging that, 'in the agonised womb of consciousness, these polar twins should be continually struggling'. The use of foetal **imagery** suggests that people are born with both instincts but one is more dominant than the other.

Even though Dr Jekyll chooses goodness, after being horrified by Mr Hyde's actions, he is constantly tempted to return to evil and eventually gives in to this temptation.

The fact that the transformations into Mr Hyde then become involuntary suggest that, once released, Dr Jekyll's evil side is stronger than his good. His Christian values ('I find it in my heart to pity him') seem no match for Mr Hyde's immorality ('scrawling in my own hand blasphemies').

Key Quotations to Learn

About Mr Hyde: … tales came out of the man's cruelty, at once so callous and violent; of his vile life, of his strange associates, (Chapter 6)

About Dr Jekyll away from Mr Hyde's influence: … his face seemed to open and brighten, as if with an inward consciousness of service; (Chapter 6)

Dr Jekyll describing his behaviour as Mr Hyde: 'I gnashed my teeth upon him with a gust of devilish fury;' (Chapter 9)

Summary

- Evil is presented through Mr Hyde, just as goodness is presented through Dr Jekyll.
- Utterson, Lanyon, Enfield and Poole display goodness and Christian values.
- Dr Jekyll conveys the internal conflict between good and evil behaviour.
- Although he ultimately chooses to be good, it is suggested that the evil impulse is stronger as Mr Hyde eventually takes over.

Sample Analysis

In Chapter 10, Stevenson explores evil through Dr Jekyll's explanation of the sensations of being Mr Hyde. Metaphors are used to describe his feelings of 'a fancy brimming with images of terror, a soul boiling with causeless hatreds', with the abstract nouns – particularly the pluralisation of 'hatreds' – conveying the absence of goodness. By mentioning the 'soul', Stevenson presents the depth of Mr Hyde's evil and the accompanying use of 'boiling' could link to the fires of Hell to imply damnation. This depiction of evil can be explored further through the adjective 'causeless', suggesting it is an instinct rather than something built on motive.

Questions

QUICK TEST
1. What three aspects of characterisation convey Mr Hyde's evil nature?
2. What biblical language is used to link Mr Hyde to evil?
3. What idea about good and evil does Stevenson explore in the novel?
4. What happens to show that Mr Hyde is taking control of Dr Jekyll's body?

EXAM PRACTICE
Using one or more of the 'Key Quotations to Learn', write a paragraph analysing how Stevenson presents goodness and/or evil.

Respectability and Repression

You must be able to: analyse how Stevenson explores the themes of respectability and repression.

How are characters presented as being respectable?

The majority of the characters follow social codes of respectability: having a clear sense of how one should behave. This was typical of the Victorian period in which the novel is set.

Mr Enfield has a rule about undue curiosity, which Mr Utterson refers to as 'a good rule'. The lawyer also says, 'I am ashamed of my long tongue', to show his awareness that he has broken a code of social politeness by discussing Mr Hyde too much.

Similar codes of courtesy can be seen in the way characters behave in contrast to Mr Hyde. Mr Utterson reprimands his aggressive speech, saying 'that is not fitting language', and Dr Lanyon encourages more gentlemanly behaviour when he offers, 'Be seated, if you please' despite his visitor's disturbing manner.

Dr Lanyon and Dr Jekyll's respectability is also presented through their servants. The former's butler is described as 'solemn' and efficient, while Poole is respectful and attentive, 'Will you wait here by the fire, sir? Or shall I give you a light in the dining room?'

What is repression and how is it presented?

Repression is the restraining of someone or something. In the novel, several characters remain respectable by repressing certain desires, such as Mr Utterson who avoids going to the theatre because it was considered **vulgar**.

The main representation of repression is Dr Jekyll. In Chapter 10, he describes how, from an early age, he struggled to repress his desires and, instead, hid his undignified pleasures to safeguard his 'honourable and distinguished future'.

A lack of repression is described negatively, using the metaphor, 'I laid aside restraint and plunged in shame'. However, metaphor is also used to describe repression as painful, 'suffer smartingly in the fires of abstinence'. Stevenson presents these contrasting images as Dr Jekyll's motivation to try to hide his dishonourable side in a separate identity.

Stevenson implies that repression is unhealthy and can make the situation worse. Dr Jekyll's attempt to resist the temptations that Mr Hyde allows only results in 'a more furious propensity to ill' when he once more drinks the transforming potion.

Stevenson emphasises this link between Dr Jekyll's repression and his downfall when he reflects on his life after the murder of Sir Danvers Carew, 'I saw my life as a whole: [...] through the self-denying toils of my professional life, to arrive again and again [...] at the damned horrors of the evening'.

Key Quotations to Learn

... the mark of a modest man ... (Chapter 1)

... my pleasures were (to say the least) undignified, and I was not only well known and highly considered, but growing towards the elderly man ... (Dr Jekyll: Chapter 10)

... I began to be tortured with throes and longings ... (Dr Jekyll: Chapter 10)

Summary

- Respectability is shown through the different codes of behaviour that the characters display.
- These codes are presented as social norms and expectations.
- Stevenson explores the idea of repression through Dr Jekyll.
- Dr Jekyll represses and hides his desires in order to maintain an appearance of respectability but this ends up destroying his life.

Sample Analysis

When Dr Jekyll describes his attempts to resist Mr Hyde in Chapter 10, 'as the first edge of my penitence wore off, the lower side of me, so long indulged, so recently chained down, began to growl for license', Stevenson uses **zoomorphism** to present repression as a moral struggle. His desires are compared with a restricted wild animal desperate for release. The necessity to repress these desires is explained through them being 'lower', while his respectable side is linked to Christian virtues through the word 'penitence'. The repetition of the intensifier 'so' helps to convey Dr Jekyll's yearning to sin but the parallelism also raises the question of whether it is the release or the repression of these desires that has worsened the situation.

Questions

QUICK TEST
1. What different behaviours suggest respectability in the novel?
2. How is Mr Hyde presented as lacking respectability?
3. In what way does Mr Utterson repress himself?
4. What contrasting feelings does Dr Jekyll have about repression?

EXAM PRACTICE
Using one or more of the 'Key Quotations to Learn', write a paragraph analysing how Stevenson presents respectability and/or repression.

Science and Discovery

You must be able to: analyse how Stevenson explores the themes of science and discovery.

How are Dr Jekyll's science experiments presented mysteriously?

Dr Lanyon's exploration of Dr Jekyll's chemicals creates mystery around his work.

Stevenson uses different senses when describing the, 'blood-red liquor, which was highly pungent to the sense of smell', but its actual identity is kept unknown and the doctor adds, 'At the other ingredients I could make no guess'. Dr Jekyll's diary of experiments is also obscure, ending 'quite abruptly' and including unusual notes such as 'total failure!'

Stevenson engages the reader by only hinting at the unusual nature of Dr Jekyll's experiments and this narrative hook is voiced by Dr Lanyon when he comments, 'All this, though it whetted my curiosity, told me little that was definite'.

A range of verbs and colours are used as Mr Hyde prepares the potion, for example, just before the transformation scene, to create a spellbinding atmosphere: melted, brighten, effervesce, changed, faded; reddish, dark purple, watery green. The 'small fumes of vapour' and the description of the potion bubbling also emphasise the eerie mood.

How is scientific discovery presented as dangerous?

In the final chapter of the novel Dr Jekyll describes the danger of his experiments, 'I knew well that I risked death'. Metaphor is used to describe the power of his drugs, 'shook the very fortress of identity' and the actual transformation is made to sound extremely painful.

Dr Lanyon also describes the transformation in a frightening way, 'staring with injected eyes, gasping with open mouth', using verbs and adjectives to suggest a violent alteration of normal physical features.

However, the greatest danger is Dr Jekyll's inability to control his transformations into Mr Hyde. Similes are used, initially to suggest that his creation is not a problem, 'Edward Hyde would pass away like the stain of breath on a mirror', then to show Dr Jekyll's horror when he changes involuntarily, 'terror woke up in my breast as sudden and startling as the crash of cymbals'.

How are Dr Jekyll's scientific discoveries presented as blasphemous?

Dr Jekyll's experiments release something abominable and diabolical in the shape of Mr Hyde. Stevenson uses metaphor to describe him as a 'child of Hell' whose 'evil was written broadly and plainly on the face'.

Meeting Mr Utterson after witnessing the transformation, Dr Lanyon refers to Dr Jekyll as an 'accursed topic'. Later, exploring the laboratory, Mr Utterson is shocked to find a religious book that Dr Jekyll has 'annotated in his own hand with startling blasphemies'.

Key Quotations to Learn

Mr Hyde describing the effects of his potion: '... a new province of knowledge and new avenues to fame and power shall be laid open to you ...' (Chapter 9)

... his face became suddenly black, and the features seemed to melt and alter ... (Dr Lanyon: Chapter 9)

I was slowly losing hold of my original and better self, and becoming slowly incorporated with my second and worse. (Dr Jekyll: Chapter 10)

Summary

- Stevenson engages the reader by using different techniques to surround Dr Jekyll's experiments with mystery.
- Later in the novel, he presents Dr Jekyll's discoveries as dangerous through images of pain and the way the transformations cannot be controlled.
- Dr Jekyll's scientific work is linked to evil and Hell to suggest that it is ungodly.

Sample Analysis

After killing Sir Danvers Carew, Dr Jekyll realises the evil results of his scientific discoveries. Taking the potion, he describes how 'The pangs of transformation had not done tearing him before Henry Jekyll, with streaming tears of gratitude and remorse, had fallen upon his knees and lifted his clasped hands to God', with this image of prayer symbolising a desire for forgiveness. With dual images appearing throughout the novel, the reference to God also indicates that Mr Hyde is satanic. The dangers of Dr Jekyll's work appear in his physical pain, shown through the noun 'pangs' and the violent verb 'tearing'. This danger is emphasised through the threat of losing his identity, which is implied when, despite Stevenson writing in the first person, Dr Jekyll refers to himself in the third person (using 'him' and 'Henry Jekyll' instead of me and I).

Questions

QUICK TEST
1. What information does Stevenson withhold in order to make Dr Jekyll's experiments seem mysterious?
2. What is the biggest danger to Dr Jekyll when he creates Mr Hyde?
3. How does Dr Jekyll's attitude towards his transformation into Mr Hyde change?
4. What does Mr Hyde do that indicates he is godless?

EXAM PRACTICE
Using one or more of the 'Key Quotations to Learn', write a paragraph analysing how Stevenson presents different attitudes towards Dr Jekyll's scientific discoveries.

Dilemmas and Consequences

You must be able to: analyse how Stevenson explores the themes of dilemma and consequence.

What dilemmas do characters face and how are these presented?

A dilemma is a difficult decision, often where the alternatives are undesirable.

In Chapter 10, Dr Jekyll describes the initial dilemma of whether to take the drug that he has created. Abstract nouns are used to present the pros ('discovery') and cons ('death') of continuing with his experiment. His dilemma is solved when he gives in to 'temptation'.

Similarly, after the first involuntary transformation into Mr Hyde, Jekyll faces the dilemma of whether to give up the drug completely. Stevenson uses an image of 'scales' to show Dr Jekyll weighing up his choices. He realises that this is a choice between good and evil; after breaking his vow not to take the drug again, he refers to it as a 'moral weakness'.

Mr Utterson also faces a moral dilemma in Chapter 5 about whether to hand Mr Hyde's letter to the police (as it could incriminate Dr Jekyll) and this increases when he discovers that it is a forgery. The metaphor 'struggled with himself' shows his reluctance to know the truth about his friend. After Mr Utterson locks the letter away in his safe, Stevenson adds the metaphor 'And his blood ran cold in his veins'. This shows Mr Utterson's horror at Dr Jekyll's behaviour but could also be interpreted as describing his own feelings about hiding the truth.

How does Stevenson present the consequences of Dr Jekyll's experiments?

Dr Jekyll faces the loss of his life as a consequence of his actions. At first, this is described as 'the terrors of the scaffold' because, if caught, Mr Hyde would be hanged for murder.

Stevenson later presents this loss of life more metaphorically as Mr Hyde takes control. The civilised Victorian gentleman cannot stop his own de-evolution and faces life as a sinful, hunted criminal.

As well as describing the 'torments' that he receives from his own creation, Dr Jekyll says how running out of the required drug has 'finally severed me from my own face and nature'.

The horror and desperation his involuntary transformations cause him can be seen when Mr Hyde goes to Dr Lanyon (who also pays the consequence for witnessing the truth) for help and is described as being 'on fire with sombre excitement'. The fire metaphor conveys his agitation and suffering as well as adding a moral element when interpreted as a link to Hell and damnation.

Key Quotations to Learn

... the terms of this debate are as old and commonplace as man; much the same inducements and alarms cast the die for any tempted and trembling sinner; (Dr Jekyll: Chapter 10)

... my punishment might have gone on for years, but for the last calamity which has now fallen, (Dr Jekyll: Chapter 10)

... the doom that is closing on us both ... (Dr Jekyll: Chapter 10)

Summary

- Dr Jekyll has the dilemma of whether to take the drug he has created and then whether to continue transforming into Mr Hyde.
- Having the dilemma of whether to show the police the incriminating letter forged by Dr Jekyll, Mr Utterson locks it in his safe.
- As a consequence of his experiments, Dr Jekyll faces the consequence of losing his identity to Mr Hyde.
- Dr Lanyon falls ill with shock and dies as a consequence of discovering the truth about Dr Jekyll's experiments.

Sample Analysis

Written retrospectively in the first person, Stevenson's final chapter explores Dr Jekyll's scientific dilemma and its consequences. Reflecting on the choice that faced him, he uses the metaphor 'That night I had come to the fatal crossroads' to show the different paths that his life could have taken. By referring to night-time, Stevenson could be using darkness to symbolise the immoral nature of Dr Jekyll's dilemma about taking the drug. The adjective 'fatal' suggests the gravity of this dilemma, as well as conveying how, in hindsight, he realises that the decision he made has brought about his downfall.

Questions

QUICK TEST
1. Why did Dr Jekyll have a dilemma about first taking the drug he had created?
2. How is Mr Utterson's dilemma about the letter one of morality?
3. In what different ways is death presented as the consequence of Dr Jekyll's experiments?

EXAM PRACTICE
Using one or more of the 'Key Quotations to Learn', write a paragraph analysing how Stevenson presents Dr Jekyll's feelings about the choices he has made.

Duality

You must be able to: analyse how Stevenson explores the theme of duality.

What is duality?

Duality refers to how two things are linked or how something consists of two parts (often in opposition to each other). Stevenson uses images of duality and doubles throughout the novel.

These images foreshadow the revelation that Mr Hyde is actually a part of Dr Jekyll, as well as allowing Stevenson to explore his belief that elements of Victorian society were hypocritical and hid their own misdemeanours while condemning them in others.

Because it is such a dominant motif in the novel, it is advisable to look back over character, setting and theme, paying specific attention to duality.

Where does Stevenson present duality in character?

Dr Jekyll and Mr Hyde are presented as two people inhabiting the same body and fighting for dominance. Dr Jekyll is well-educated, respectable, charitable and Christian; Mr Hyde is barbarous, criminal, aggressive and blasphemous. Hyde's otherness contrasts with Jekyll's apparent normality.

The contrast between Jekyll's double identities is conveyed particularly well in chapter 10 by detailed comparison of their hands. The doctor's hands are 'large, firm, white, and comely' whereas Hyde's hands are 'lean, corded, knuckly, of a dusky pallor and thickly shaded with a swarthy growth of hair'.

Mr Utterson and Dr Jekyll are presented as dual aspects of Victorian society. They both have similar social status and good reputation, but the lawyer represses temptation and lives a life of moderation, while his friend secretly indulges all his sinful desires. The same link could be made between Dr Jekyll and Dr Lanyon.

How is duality presented through settings?

There is duality in the symbolic way Dr Jekyll's house is described. The front entrance looks welcoming, affluent and well-kept, while the back entrance that is used by Mr Hyde is unwelcoming, sinister and neglected.

This is developed further when Stevenson describes Mr Hyde's lodgings in Soho. The streets outside are dirty, full of poverty and linked to a lack of morality: 'his blackguardly surroundings'. However, the interior is luxurious, well-decorated and respectable: 'the plate was of silver, the napery elegant'.

Which themes of the novel also link to duality?

Duality is a theme in itself but Stevenson includes other themes that contain aspects of doubling. For example, he explores good and evil, the dilemmas that characters face and the way in which characters repress their true natures and present a false impression to society.

Key Quotations to Learn

'My master [...] is a tall, fine build of a man, and this was more of a dwarf.' (Poole: Chapter 8)

... those provinces of good and ill that divide and compound man's dual nature. (Dr Jekyll: Chapter 10)

... two natures that contended in the field of my consciousness, (Dr Jekyll: Chapter 10)

Summary

- Duality is a recurring motif throughout the novel that can be seen in Stevenson's characters, settings and themes.
- Dr Jekyll and Mr Hyde are the main image of duality and this is particularly explored in Chapter 10.
- Specific images are used to convey duality, such as the difference between the front and back of Dr Jekyll's house, the contrasting interior and exterior of Mr Hyde's lodgings and the differences between the two men's hands.

Sample Analysis

Stevenson explores duality when Dr Jekyll relates his view that, 'all human beings, as we meet them, are commingled out of good and evil' to explain his conflicting nature. The juxtaposing of two contrasting abstract nouns emphasises the idea that Jekyll and Hyde are two opposing aspects of the same person. The verb 'commingled' suggests that, usually, these opposites are blended together in one form and this is highlighted by the noun phrase 'all human beings'. Through this, Stevenson attacks those members of Victorian society who presented themselves as morally perfect and beyond reproach.

Questions

QUICK TEST
1. How are images of duality used to foreshadow events in the novel?
2. What is different between the main entrance to Dr Jekyll's house and the entrance used by Mr Hyde?
3. What is oddly contrasting about Mr Hyde's lodgings?

EXAM PRACTICE
Using one or more of the 'Key Quotations to Learn', write a paragraph analysing how Stevenson presents the theme of duality in the novel.

Tips and Assessment Objectives

You must be able to: understand how to approach the exam question and meet the requirements of the mark scheme.

Quick Tips

- You will get a choice of two questions. Choose the one that best matches your knowledge, the quotations you have learned and the things you have revised.

- Make sure you know what the question is asking you. Underline key words and pay particular attention to the bullet point prompts that come with the question.

- You should spend about 45 minutes on your *Dr Jekyll and Mr Hyde* response. Allow yourself five minutes to plan your answer so there is some structure to your essay.

- All your paragraphs should contain a clear idea, a relevant reference to the novel (ideally a quotation) and analysis of how Stevenson conveys this idea. Whenever possible, you should link your comments to the novel's context.

- It can sometimes help, after each paragraph, to quickly re-read the question to keep yourself focussed on the exam task.

- Keep your writing concise. If you waste time 'waffling' you won't be able to include the full range of analysis and understanding that the mark scheme requires.

- It is a good idea to remember what the mark scheme is asking of you...

AO1: Understand and respond to the novel (12 marks)

This is all about coming up with a range of points that match the question, supporting your ideas with references from the novel and writing your essay in a mature, academic style.

Lower	Middle	Upper
The essay has some good ideas that are mostly relevant. Some quotations and references are used to support the ideas.	A clear essay that always focusses on the exam question. Quotations and references support ideas effectively. The response refers to different points in the novel.	A convincing, well-structured essay that answers the question fully. Quotations and references are well-chosen and integrated into sentences. The response covers the whole novel (not everything, but ideas from different sections rather than just focussing on one or two chapters).

AO2: Analyse effects of Stevenson's language, form, and structure (12 marks)

You need to comment on how specific words, language techniques, sentence structures or the narrative structure allow Stevenson to get his ideas across to the reader. This could simply be something about a character or a larger idea he is exploring through the novel. To achieve this, you will need to have learned good quotations to analyse.

Lower	Middle	Upper
Identification of some different methods used by Stevenson to convey meaning. Some subject terminology.	Explanation of Stevenson's different methods. Clear understanding of the effects of these methods. Accurate use of subject terminology.	Analysis of the full range of Stevenson's methods. Thorough exploration of the effects of these methods. Accurate range of subject terminology.

AO3: Understand the relationship between the novel and its contexts (6 marks)

For this part of the mark scheme, you need to show your understanding of how the characters or Stevenson's ideas relate to when he was writing (1886) and the novel's setting (nineteenth century).

Lower	Middle	Upper
Some awareness of how ideas in the novel link to its context.	References to relevant aspects of context show clear understanding.	Exploration is linked to specific aspects of the novel's contexts to show detailed understanding.

AO4: Written accuracy (4 marks)

You need to use accurate vocabulary, expression, punctuation and spelling. Although it's only four marks, this could make the difference between a lower or a higher grade.

Lower	Middle	Upper
Reasonable level of accuracy. Errors do not get in the way of the essay making sense.	Good level of accuracy. Vocabulary and sentences help to keep ideas clear.	Consistent high level of accuracy. Vocabulary and sentences are used to make ideas clear and precise.

Practice Questions

1. What do you think is the importance of the first chapter of *Dr Jekyll and Mr Hyde*?

   Write about:

   • how the opening of the novel presents some important ideas

   • how Stevenson presents these ideas by the ways he writes.

2. How does Stevenson use the character of Henry Jekyll to explore ideas about morality in *Dr Jekyll and Mr Hyde*?

   Write about:

   • how Stevenson presents Henry Jekyll

   • how Stevenson uses Henry Jekyll to explore some of his ideas.

3. How does Stevenson present ideas about duality in *Dr Jekyll and Mr Hyde*?

   Write about:

   • how Stevenson links characters and setting to duality

   • how Stevenson explores duality in the novel.

4. 'In *Dr Jekyll and Mr Hyde*, it is difficult to sympathise with Henry Jekyll'. Explore how far you agree with this statement.

   Write about:

   • how Stevenson presents the character of Henry Jekyll

   • how Stevenson uses the character of Henry Jekyll to explore some of his ideas.

5. How does Stevenson present attitudes about reputation in *Dr Jekyll and Mr Hyde*?

   Write about:

   • what some of the attitudes about reputation are

   • how Stevenson presents some of these attitudes by the ways he writes.

6. 'Mr Utterson is presented as a good Victorian gentleman in *Dr Jekyll and Mr Hyde*'. Explore how far you agree with this statement.

   Write about:

   • how Stevenson presents the character of Mr Utterson

   • how Stevenson uses the character of Mr Utterson to explore some of his ideas.

7. How does Stevenson create an atmosphere of mystery in *Dr Jekyll and Mr Hyde*?

   Write about:

   • the ways Stevenson uses characters and settings to create mystery

   • how Stevenson structures his novel to create mystery.

8. How does Stevenson present Mr Hyde as a monstrous character in *Dr Jekyll and Mr Hyde*?

   Write about:

   • the ways Mr Hyde looks, behaves and speaks

   • how Stevenson presents Mr Hyde in the novel.

9. In *Dr Jekyll and Mr Hyde*, Dr Lanyon refers to Henry Jekyll's work as 'unscientific balderdash'. How does Stevenson explore attitudes towards science?

Write about:

- how Stevenson presents attitudes towards science
- how Stevenson uses these attitudes to explore ideas about society.

10. How does Stevenson present inner conflict in *Dr Jekyll and Mr Hyde*?

Write about:

- the different types of inner conflict displayed in the novel
- how Stevenson presents inner conflict.

11. *Dr Jekyll and Mr Hyde* has been described as 'a horror story about society'. To what extent do you agree with this view?

Write about:

- how Stevenson presents horror
- how Stevenson uses horror to explore some of his ideas about society.

12. In *Dr Jekyll and Mr Hyde*, how does Stevenson present some of the differences between Henry Jekyll and Edward Hyde?

Write about:

- how Stevenson presents differences between Henry Jekyll and Edward Hyde
- how Stevenson uses these differences to explore ideas about humankind.

13. At the start of *Dr Jekyll and Mr Hyde*, Mr Enfield compares Edward Hyde to Satan. How does Stevenson present ideas about evil in the novel?

Write about:

- what some of the ideas about evil are
- how Stevenson presents these ideas by the ways he writes.

14. How does Stevenson present the relationship between Mr Utterson and Henry Jekyll in *Dr Jekyll and Mr Hyde*?

Write about:

- what Mr Utterson and Henry Jekyll's relationship is like
- how Stevenson presents their relationship by the ways he writes.

15. How does Stevenson use his characters to explore ideas about repression in *Dr Jekyll and Mr Hyde*?

Write about:

- how Stevenson presents ideas about repression
- how Stevenson uses his characters to explore some of his ideas.

16. *Dr Jekyll and Mr Hyde* has been described as 'a novel about decisions and consequences'. To what extent do you agree with this view?

Write about:

- how Stevenson presents decisions and consequences
- how Stevenson uses decisions and consequences to explore some of his ideas about society.

17. How does Stevenson use settings to explore characters in *Dr Jekyll and Mr Hyde*?

Write about:

- how Stevenson presents different settings
- how Stevenson uses his settings to explore ideas about characters and society.

18. 'Mr Hyde is an unusual villain'. Explore how far you agree with this statement.

Write about:

- how Stevenson presents the character of Mr Hyde
- how Stevenson uses the character of Mr Hyde to explore some of his ideas.

Planning a Character Question Response

You must be able to: understand what an exam question is asking you and prepare your response.

How might an exam question on character be phrased?

A typical character question will read like this:

How does Stevenson present Edward Hyde's attitudes towards others in *Dr Jekyll and Mr Hyde*? Write about:

- how Mr Hyde responds to other characters in the novel
- how Stevenson presents Mr Hyde by the ways he writes.

[30 marks + 4 AO4 marks]

How do I work out what to do?

The focus of this question is clear: Mr Hyde and his attitudes towards others.

'How' is an important element of this question.

For AO1, this word shows that you need to display a clear understanding of what Mr Hyde is like in terms of his attitudes to others and the reasons for these attitudes.

For AO2, 'how' makes it clear that you need to analyse the different ways in which Stevenson's use of language, structure and form help to show the reader Mr Hyde's attitudes to others. Ideally, you should include quotations you have learnt but, if necessary, you can make a clear reference to a specific part of the novel.

You also need to remember to link your comments to the novel's context to achieve your AO3 marks and write accurately to pick up your four AO4 marks for spelling, punctuation and grammar.

How can I plan my essay?

You have approximately 45 minutes to write your essay.

This isn't long but you should spend the first five minutes writing a quick plan. This will help you to focus your thoughts and produce a well-structured essay.

Try to come up with five or six ideas. Each of these ideas can then be written up as a paragraph.

You can plan in whatever way you find most useful. Some students like to just make a quick list of points and then re-number them into a logical order. Spider diagrams are particularly popular; look at the example on the opposite page.

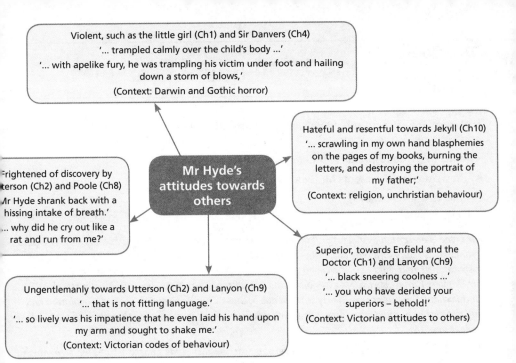

Violent, such as the little girl (Ch1) and Sir Danvers (Ch4)
'... trampled calmly over the child's body ...'
'... with apelike fury, he was trampling his victim under foot and hailing down a storm of blows,'
(Context: Darwin and Gothic horror)

Mr Hyde's attitudes towards others

Hateful and resentful towards Jekyll (Ch10)
'... scrawling in my own hand blasphemies on the pages of my books, burning the letters, and destroying the portrait of my father;'
(Context: religion, unchristian behaviour)

Frightened of discovery by [U]terson (Ch2) and Poole (Ch8)
[M]r Hyde shrank back with a hissing intake of breath.'
'... why did he cry out like a rat and run from me?'

Superior, towards Enfield and the Doctor (Ch1) and Lanyon (Ch9)
'... black sneering coolness ...'
'... you who have derided your superiors – behold!'
(Context: Victorian attitudes to others)

Ungentlemanly towards Utterson (Ch2) and Lanyon (Ch9)
'... that is not fitting language.'
'... so lively was his impatience that he even laid his hand upon my arm and sought to shake me.'
(Context: Victorian codes of behaviour)

Summary

- Make sure you know what the focus of the essay is.
- Remember to analyse how ideas are conveyed by Stevenson.
- Try to relate your ideas to the novel's social, historical and literary context.

Questions

QUICK TEST
1. What key skills do you need to show in your answer?
2. What are the benefits of quickly planning your essay?
3. Why is it better to have learned quotations for the exam?

EXAM PRACTICE
Plan a response to the following exam question:

How does Stevenson present Henry Jekyll's attitudes towards others in *Dr Jekyll and Mr Hyde*?

Write about:
- how Dr Jekyll responds to other characters in the novel
- how Stevenson presents Dr Jekyll by the ways he writes.

[30 marks + 4 AO4 marks]

How does Stevenson present Edward Hyde's attitudes towards others in *Dr Jekyll and Mr Hyde*? Write about:

• how Mr Hyde responds to other characters in the novel

• how Stevenson presents Mr Hyde by the ways he writes.

[30 marks + 4 AO4 marks]

Mr Hyde is presented as violent and unfeeling: 'trampled calmly over the child's body' (1). The word 'trampled' is really different to 'calmly' and this suggests that Mr Hyde doesn't care that he has just stamped on a child (2). Stevenson uses a similar description when Mr Hyde attacks and kills Sir Danvers Carew. He uses really violent and horrible words to show how vicious the attack is (3). In this chapter, he compares Mr Hyde to an ape because Charles Darwin's theory of evolution had suggested that humans were descended from monkeys. So he is suggesting that we're all just violent apes (4).

Mr Hyde hates and resents Dr Jekyll. Stevenson describes Mr Hyde's nasty actions as: 'scrawling in my own hand blasphemies on the pages of my books, burning the letters, and destroying the portrait of my father' (5). This is a list (6). The verbs sound aggressive, which gets across the idea that Mr Hyde hates Dr Jekyll. The things he does are also personal attacks on Dr Jekyll. 'Blasphemies' means swearing about God so Mr Hyde is attacking his religion and religion was important in the nineteenth century. 'The letters' could mean that Dr Jekyll has friends but Mr Hyde wants him to feel as lonely as he is. And 'father' means his dad, which suggests that Mr Hyde doesn't respect Dr Jekyll's family, even though Dr Jekyll is a gentleman so he would have had a respectable family (7). This links to Victorian values (8).

Mr Hyde acts like he is better than other people. When he is captured by Enfield and the doctor in Chapter 1, he pulls a face to suggest that he doesn't like the other people and doesn't care what they think of him. Similarly, when he goes to Dr Lanyon's house he calls himself Dr Lanyon's 'superior'. It is odd that he thinks he is better than other people because he is small and disgusting to look at. Stevenson might be suggesting that this is what the Victorians were really like. They thought they were brilliant and looked down on people but really they were disgusting, they just hid all their disgusting stuff away so people didn't know. This was hypocritical (9).

In the nineteenth century, there were Victorian values. This meant being polite to other people, dressing well, and having a good reputation. Stevenson shows that Mr Hyde doesn't have Victorian values because he doesn't act like a gentleman when he meets other people. In Chapter 2, when he first meets Mr Utterson he loses his temper and calls Mr Utterson a liar. Mr Utterson tells him off and says his behaviour is ungentlemanly: 'that is not fitting language'. Fitting is an adjective and Stevenson uses it to show that Mr Hyde's behaviour does not fit into what is expected in society (10). He also gets told off by Dr Lanyon when he doesn't behave appropriately as a guest in

Dr Lanyon's house. He is very excited and grabs hold of Dr Lanyon. Dr Lanyon has to calm him down and tells him to sit down so they can talk like gentlemen.

Although he's usually scary and aggressive, Mr Hyde is scared by others when he thinks he's in danger. Poole says 'cry out like a rat and run from me' and when he meets Mr Utterson he 'shrank back with a hissing intake of breath'. He does this because he does not know who Mr Utterson is. The phrase 'shrank back' shows he is a bit scared. But when he hisses it also sounds like a snake and snakes do this to warn people off (11).

1. The opening sentence establishes a clear point. This is supported by a relevant quotation but it could be embedded. AO1

2. There is some explanation of how language shows Mr Hyde's attitude. Subject terminology could be incorporated. AO2

3. The first point is developed. There is a vague suggestion of patterns of language but the lack of a quotation means this cannot be explored. AO1/AO2

4. There is some attempt to use historical context to explain Stevenson's language choices but greater clarity is needed. AO1/AO3

5. A new point is established and a relevant quotation is used as evidence. Again, this would be better if the quotation was embedded. AO1

6. Stevenson's use of sentence structure is identified but not analysed. AO2

7. Some subject terminology is used and there is some good analysis of language. However, the writing could be more concise and sophisticated. AO1/AO2/AO4

8. Historical context is included but it is just tagged on rather than being linked to the analysis. AO3

9. There is an attempt to use some sophisticated language but the previous sentence is too **informal** and repetitive. AO1

10. Although it could be written with greater precision and sophistication, there is some clear analysis of language linked to social context. AO1/AO2/AO3

11. Quotations are beginning to be embedded. There is some good analysis of language but the first of the two quotations are ignored. AO1/AO2

> ## Questions
>
> EXAM PRACTICE
> Choose a paragraph of this essay. Read it through a few times then try to rewrite and improve it. You might:
> * Improve the sophistication of the language or the clarity of expression.
> * Replace a reference with a quotation or use a better quotation.
> * Provide more detailed, or a wider range of, analysis.
> * Use more subject terminology.
> * Link some context to the analysis more effectively.

Grade 7+ Annotated Response

A proportion of the best top-band answers will be awarded Grade 8 or Grade 9. To achieve this, you should aim for a sophisticated, fluid and nuanced response that displays flair and originality.

How does Stevenson present Edward Hyde's attitudes towards others in *Dr Jekyll and Mr Hyde*? Write about:

- how Mr Hyde responds to other characters in the novel
- how Stevenson presents Mr Hyde by the ways he writes.   [30 marks + 4 AO4 marks]

One of the most striking aspects of Mr Hyde's attitudes toward others is his violent callousness. Creating a shocking situation as part of his urban Gothic horror, Stevenson describes how Mr Hyde 'trampled calmly over the child's body' as if it did not matter (1). The brutal verb contrasts with the adverb to suggest that he is utterly indifferent to others (2). Stevenson includes the same verb, 'with apelike fury, he was trampling his victim under foot and hailing down a storm of blows', when Sir Danvers is attacked. The abstract noun and the metaphor emphasise the extent of Mr Hyde's violent attitude (3). As well as this being part of his novel's genre, Stevenson is exploring the nature of humankind. He uses the ape comparison to link to Charles Darwin's theory of evolution and to suggest that this violence is inside us all (4).

Mr Hyde seems to be a product of de-evolution and his otherness is partly what makes him resentful towards Dr Jekyll (5). Stevenson uses the list of malicious actions (6), 'scrawling in my own hand blasphemies on the pages of my books, burning the letters, and destroying the portrait of my father', to build up an image of Mr Hyde's hatred. As well as achieving this through increasingly aggressive verbs, Stevenson shows Mr Hyde attacking central aspects of Dr Jekyll's identity: religion, friends and family. This can be seen not just as an attack on his alter-ego but on the values of a society in which he has no place (7).

As well as showing bitterness towards others, Mr Hyde displays an arrogant superiority. Enfield describes his 'black sneering coolness' and he addresses Dr Lanyon with the words, 'you who have derided your superiors – behold!' before taking the transformative drug. Stevenson could be satirising the hypocrisy of the Victorians who, with their powerful empire and their outward morality, saw themselves as better than others despite their own flaws and corruption (8). The verb 'sneering' suggests this sense of contempt just as the old-fashioned **imperative** 'behold' implies a self-importance that is then highlighted by the dramatic exclamation mark (9).

Victorian values also link to Mr Hyde's ungentlemanly attitude towards others. Mr Utterson upbraids him with the comment, 'that is not fitting language', after Mr Hyde loses his temper and calls him a liar. The **adjective phrase** captures how Mr Hyde's demeanour does not match expected codes of politeness. This is developed by his attitude to Dr Lanyon, 'so lively was his impatience that he even laid his hand upon my arm and sought to shake me', after which the doctor has to remind *him of appropriate ways to behave. The adverbs 'so' and 'even' intensify Mr Hyde's lack of propriety while his agitation and aggression link back to his violent indifference to others (10).*

*Perhaps surprisingly, Mr Hyde is also presented as being frightened by other characters. This seems to stem from a fear of discovery, such as when he 'shrank back with a hissing intake of breath' upon being interrupted by Mr Utterson, or Poole's recollection that he 'cry out like a rat and run from me' when seen outside the cabinet. In both descriptions, Stevenson uses **verb phrases** to depict a scared, defensive action. He uses animal imagery to show this fear and perhaps suggests it is lowly or dishonourable. The onomatopoeic 'hissing' could also imply a snakelike wish to deter Mr Utterson, just as the rat simile may additionally show Mr Hyde's sly cunning. Here, and throughout the novel, Mr Hyde's attitude to others is sinister and at variance with contemporaneous social expectations, creating a memorably monstrous character (11).*

1. The opening sentences establish a clear point about Mr Hyde which is linked to literary context and supported by an embedded quotation. AO1/AO3

2. Analysis of language, using clear subject terminology, to show how Mr Hyde's attitude is presented. AO2

3. The first point is developed through an additional quotation and the analysis of patterns of language in Stevenson's writing. AO1/AO2

4. Historical context is used to develop the point further. AO3

5. The argument is developed by an effective transition between the paragraphs before a new point is established. AO1

6. The effect of Stevenson's sentence structure is explored to add variety to the essay's analysis. AO2

7. Analysis is developed and combined with social context. AO2/AO3

8. Social and historical context are included in order to consider how the character of Mr Hyde is being used by Stevenson. AO3

9. Language and sentence structure are analysed to develop the point being made. AO2

10. The essay refers back to previous points in order to strengthen the argument. AO1

11. The essay ends with a quick conclusive sentence that, like the rest of the essay, is well-written and contains some precise, sophisticated language. AO1/AO4

> **Questions**
>
> EXAM PRACTICE
> Spend 45 minutes writing an answer to the following question:
> How does Stevenson present Henry Jekyll's attitudes towards others in *Dr Jekyll and Mr Hyde*? Write about:
> * how Dr Jekyll responds to other characters in the novel
> * how Stevenson presents Dr Jekyll by the ways he writes.
>
> [30 marks + 4 AO4 marks]
> Remember to use the plan you have already prepared.

Planning a Theme Question Response

You must be able to: understand what an exam question is asking you and prepare your response.

How might an exam question on theme be phrased?

A typical theme question will read like this:

How does Stevenson explore ideas about good and evil in *Dr Jekyll and Mr Hyde*? Write about:

- where good and evil are presented in the novel
- how Stevenson explores ideas about good and evil by the ways he writes.

[30 marks + 4 AO4 marks]

How do I work out what to do?

The focus of this question is clear: good and evil.

'How' is an important element of this question.

For AO1, this word shows that you need to display a clear understanding of the aspects of the novel that link to good and evil.

For AO2, 'how' makes it clear that you need to analyse the different ways in which Stevenson uses language, structure and form to explore different ideas about good and evil. Ideally, you should include quotations that you have learnt but, if necessary, you can make a clear reference to a specific part of the novel.

You also need to remember to link your comments to the novel's context to achieve your AO3 marks and write accurately to pick up your four AO4 marks for spelling, punctuation and grammar.

How can I plan my essay?

You have approximately 45 minutes to write your essay.

This isn't long but you should spend the first five minutes writing a quick plan. This will help you to focus your thoughts and produce a well-structured essay.

Try to come up with five or six ideas. Each of these ideas can then be written up as a paragraph.

You can plan in whatever way you find most useful. Some students like to just make a quick list of points and then re-number them into a logical order. Spider diagrams are particularly popular; look at the example on the opposite page.

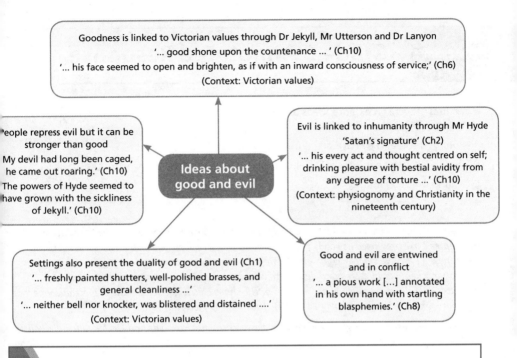

Goodness is linked to Victorian values through Dr Jekyll, Mr Utterson and Dr Lanyon
'... good shone upon the countenance ... ' (Ch10)
'... his face seemed to open and brighten, as if with an inward consciousness of service;' (Ch6)
(Context: Victorian values)

People repress evil but it can be stronger than good
My devil had long been caged, he came out roaring.' (Ch10)
The powers of Hyde seemed to have grown with the sickliness of Jekyll.' (Ch10)

Ideas about good and evil

Evil is linked to inhumanity through Mr Hyde
'Satan's signature' (Ch2)
'... his every act and thought centred on self; drinking pleasure with bestial avidity from any degree of torture ...' (Ch10)
(Context: physiognomy and Christianity in the nineteenth century)

Settings also present the duality of good and evil (Ch1)
'... freshly painted shutters, well-polished brasses, and general cleanliness ...'
'... neither bell nor knocker, was blistered and distained ....'
(Context: Victorian values)

Good and evil are entwined and in conflict
'... a pious work [...] annotated in his own hand with startling blasphemies.' (Ch8)

Summary

- Make sure you know what the focus of the essay is.
- Remember to analyse how ideas are conveyed by Stevenson.
- Try to relate your ideas to the novel's social, historical and literary context.

Questions

QUICK TEST
1. What key skills do you need to show in your answer?
2. What are the benefits of quickly planning your essay?
3. Why is it better to have learned quotations for the exam?

EXAM PRACTICE
Plan a response to the following exam question:

How does Stevenson explore ideas about reputation in *Dr Jekyll and Mr Hyde*?

Write about:
- where reputation is presented in the novel
- how Stevenson presents ideas about reputation by the ways he writes.
[30 marks + 4 AO4 marks]

Grade 5 Annotated Response

How does Stevenson explore ideas about good and evil in *Dr Jekyll and Mr Hyde*?
Write about:

- where good and evil are presented in the novel
- how Stevenson explores ideas about good and evil by the ways he writes.

[30 marks + 4 AO4 marks]

One way in which good and evil is presented is through opposite descriptions of setting. The shops in Chapter 1 are presented as good, 'freshly painted shutters, well-polished brasses, and general cleanliness' (1). However, Mr Hyde's back-entrance to the laboratory is presented as evil, 'neither bell nor knocker, was blistered and distained'. Words such as 'cleanliness' and 'distained' are opposites, just like good and evil are opposites. The shops also look friendly and respectable whereas the door looks unfriendly and disgusting (2). This links to Victorian values (3).

The characters also suggest good and evil. Stevenson presents Mr Hyde and Dr Jekyll using duality to show that good and evil are opposites (4). Hyde's 'every act and thought centred on self; drinking pleasure with bestial avidity from any degree of torture', which makes him sound evil (5). Stevenson adds to this when he describes Mr Hyde's face as having Satan's name on it. This is a metaphor. This links to the time the book was written because in the nineteenth century everyone was Christian and believed in God. This means that Mr Hyde would have seemed really evil (6).

In contrast, Dr Jekyll seems good, 'good shone upon the countenance'. This says that Dr Jekyll was a good person and you could tell by looking at him. Stevenson uses light, which can symbolise God. So Mr Hyde was evil but Dr Jekyll was good. This is also called physiognomy where the Victorians believed you could tell what someone was like from their face. We are also told that he is religious and does loads of charitable work. This is different to Mr Hyde who was described as being selfish. Being charitable is also a Christian thing which reinforces the idea that Dr Jekyll is good but Mr Hyde is evil (7).

Stevenson writes about good and evil as if they are in a battle to control Dr Jekyll (8). A good example of this is where Mr Utterson discovers one of Dr Jekyll's books in Chapter 8, 'a pious work [...] annotated in his own hand with startling blasphemies'. The word 'pious' is an adjective meaning religious, which reminds the reader that Dr Jekyll is good. However, 'blasphemies' is when you swear and insult God which shows that Mr Hyde is evil. Importantly, Stevenson uses the word 'annotated' and this means notetaking so Mr Hyde has written over the religious stuff which symbolises that evil is more powerful than good. Mr Utterson finds this 'startling'. This is another adjective and it emphasises how evil Mr Hyde seems (9).

Stevenson continues to describe how evil is a stronger force than good when Dr Jekyll describes what Mr Hyde is like, 'My devil had long been caged, he came out roaring'. The words 'devil' and 'roaring' make Mr Hyde sound evil. This is another example of Stevenson using language, such as with Satan (10). It also makes Mr Hyde sound scary and violent whereas Dr Jekyll tries to be nice. Because he tried to keep Mr Hyde 'caged' this links to something called repression. The Victorians tried to do this rather than being honest about their feelings so Stevenson is saying that isn't a good thing. It makes the problem worse. At the end, evil has taken over. Dr Jekyll can't stop the transformation into Mr Hyde and it describes, 'The powers of Hyde seemed to have grown with the sickliness of Jekyll'. 'Powers' and 'sickliness' are nouns and they are opposites and this shows that good and evil are opposites and evil is stronger than good (11).

1. The opening sentences establish a clear point, although it could be more subtly linked to the essay question. A relevant quotation is used as evidence but it would better if it was embedded. AO1

2. There is some attempt to analyse language but it could be more detailed and precise. Subject terminology could be used. AO2

3. A reference is made to context but it is tagged on and unexplained. AO3

4. A new point is established and some thought is given to ideas about good and evil. AO1

5. A relevant quotation is embedded into the sentence but is left without analysis. AO1/AO2

6. Some subject terminology is used (but not successfully integrated) and there is some analysis of language alongside a general but relevant reference to historical context. AO1/AO2/AO3

7. There is some good analysis of language, linked to the historical context. However, in places, the writing is a little simple and too informal. AO1/AO2/AO3

8. A new point is made that clearly links to the essay's focus of ideas about good and evil. AO1

9. Although it is a little simple and mechanical, there is some good analysis of the effects of language. AO2

10. An attempt is made to identify patterns of language used by Stevenson. AO2

11. The essay has some sense of conclusion but, like a lot of the essay, it is rather generalised. There is a lack of precision and sophistication. AO1/AO4

Questions

EXAM PRACTICE

Choose a paragraph of this essay. Read it through a few times then try to rewrite and improve it. You might:

- Improve the sophistication of the language or the clarity of expression.
- Replace a reference with a quotation or use a better quotation.
- Provide more detailed, or a wider range of, analysis.
- Use more subject terminology.
- Link some context to the analysis more effectively.

Grade 7+ Annotated Response

A proportion of the best top-band answers will be awarded Grade 8 or Grade 9. To achieve this, you should aim for a sophisticated, fluid and nuanced response that displays flair and originality.

How does Stevenson explore ideas about good and evil in *Dr Jekyll and Mr Hyde*? Write about:

- where good and evil are presented in the novel
- how Stevenson explores ideas about good and evil by the ways he writes.

[30 marks + 4 AO4 marks]

The presentation of good and evil in Dr Jekyll and Mr Hyde is more complex that it at first may seem. Initially, Stevenson creates a simple duality through the settings of Chapter 1 (1). Using the readers' expectations of horror stories, the noun phrases, 'freshly painted shutters, well-polished brasses, and general cleanliness' (2), present the shops as symbolising goodness through their reflection of the Victorian values of reputation, respectability and morality. In contrast, Mr Hyde's back-entrance to the laboratory, 'neither bell nor knocker, was blistered and distained', implies evil through images of secrecy and neglect, with the two adjectives also presenting evil as a disease (3).

Stevenson continues this duality of good and evil through his characters. Mr Hyde is used to suggest that evil is something inhuman (4), 'his every act and thought centred on self; drinking pleasure with bestial avidity from any degree of torture', describing behaviour contrary to the basic teachings of Christianity that permeated Victorian society. The animal reference suggests that evil removes, or is defined by a lack of, humanity. An image of selfishness and revelling in wrongdoing is created by combining the metaphor with the adjectives 'every' and 'any', while the contrasting nouns 'pleasure' and 'torture' add to this by implying that Mr Hyde is not just violent but gains in some way from that violence; for Hyde, it is a disturbingly sensual response (5). Stevenson also combines Christian references with nineteenth century pseudoscience when Mr Hyde is said to have 'Satan's signature' across his face. The metaphor suggests that evil is defined by a lack of Christian behaviour and that this evil is so strong it has manifested in his physical appearance (6).

In contrast, goodness is linked again to strong Victorian values through characters like Mr Utterson and Dr Jekyll. Physiognomy reappears in phrases such as 'good shone upon the countenance' and 'his face seemed to open and brighten, as if with an inward consciousness of service' to show Jekyll's reputation and morality. Both metaphors use images of light that are symbolic of God; these are emphasised by the reference to 'service' to suggest religious charity, unlike Hyde's selfishness (7). However, this duality between Dr Jekyll and Mr Hyde deepens the exploration of good and evil because the two characters are the same person: Stevenson appears to be asserting that evil can be found in anyone, regardless of how they look or behave in public (8).

This idea that good and evil are entwined is developed by presenting them as battling for supremacy. In Chapter 8, Mr Utterson discovers, 'a pious work [...] annotated in his own hand with startling blasphemies', which Stevenson uses to represent this internal conflict. The adjective 'pious' suggests Dr Jekyll's Christian values but these have been overwritten with contrasting sacrilege to imply the powerful influence of evil. The adjective 'startling' indicates Mr Utterson's shock and this could mirror what Stevenson saw as the Victorians' unwillingness to believe that evil might lurk behind their veneer of social respectability (9).

Stevenson continues to explore the idea that evil is a stronger force than good. Dr Jekyll describes how, 'My devil had long been caged, he came out roaring', after breaking his vow not to take the transformative drug. Repression is shown to fail, with the short sentence and the verb 'roaring' emphasising the brutality and power of evil (10). He uses the recurring motif of duality to describe how 'The powers of Hyde seemed to have grown with the sickliness of Jekyll', contrasting abstract nouns to present the bleak notion that evil desires can be stronger than the urge to do good (11).

1. The opening sentences introduce a sense of argument to the essay before establishing a clear point about good and evil. AO1

2. Supporting quotations are embedded into the sentences. AO1

3. Analysis of language is combined with subject terminology and literary context to explore good and evil. AO2/AO3

4. There is an effective transition between the paragraphs before a new point is established. AO1

5. Further analysis of language is combined with social context to explore good and evil. AO2/AO3

6. The point is developed through an additional quotation and analysis of language. AO1/AO2

7. Patterns of language in Stevenson's writing are explored. AO2

8. The argument is developed further. The essay does not just focus on how good and evil are shown, but responds to the question by exploring ideas about good and evil. AO1

9. The effect of Stevenson's sentence structure is explored to add variety to the essay's analysis. AO2

10. A range of analysis continues to be combined with aspects of the novel's context. AO2/AO3.

11. The essay ends with a conclusive sentence that, like the rest of the essay, is well-written and contains some precise, sophisticated language. AO1/AO4

Questions

EXAM PRACTICE

Spend 45 minutes writing an answer to the following question:

How does Stevenson explore ideas about reputation in *Dr Jekyll and Mr Hyde*?
Write about:

- where reputation is presented in the novel
- how Stevenson presents ideas about reputation by the ways he writes.

[30 marks + 4 AO4 marks]

Remember to use the plan you have already prepared.

Glossary

Abstract noun – a noun that is an idea or quality rather than a concrete object (such as: wealth, happiness).

Adjective – a word that describes a noun.

Adjective phrase – a series of words creating an adjective.

Adverb – a word that describes a verb.

Alter ego – someone's alternative personality.

Ambiguous – unclear; open to more than one interpretation.

Atmosphere – the mood or emotion in a novel.

Blasphemous – something that goes against God or the teachings of the Church.

Clause – a part of a sentence, separated by a punctuation mark.

Conjunction – a word used to connect clauses.

Contemporary – modern.

Damned – an idea that someone will go to Hell because of what they have done.

Decadent – showing moral decline through self-indulgence.

Degenerate – having lost normal moral behaviour and thought.

Dichotomy – a contrast between two opposite ideas.

Disingenuous – lacking sincerity; pretending to know less than one really does.

Duality – having two aspects or elements, often in contrast with each other.

Duplicitous – deceitful; a liar.

Evolution – the process by which life on Earth developed from earlier forms of life.

First-person narrative – a story told from the point of view of a character.

Flashback – a scene set in an earlier time to the main story.

Foreshadowing – warning about or indicating a future event.

Guilt – regret for something you have done.

Homophone – a word that has the same pronunciation, but different meaning, as another word.

Hypocritical – when someone criticises behaviour or attitudes that they themselves have.

Imagery – words used to create a picture in the imagination.

Imperative – an order.

Informal – casual or friendly.

Linear narrative – a story told in chronological order.

Metaphor – a descriptive technique, using comparison to say one thing is something else.

Mien – a person's mood shown through their appearance or manner.

Morality – a clear belief in right and wrong, good and bad.

Noun – an object or thing.

Noun phrase – a group of words making up a noun.

Ominous – threatening, suggesting something bad is going to happen.

Omniscient – all-seeing and all-knowing.

Pall – a cloth (usually black) placed over a coffin.

Parallelism – a phrase that is repeated with minor changes to emphasise an idea.

Pattern of three – three related ideas, placed together for emphasis.

Personification – writing about an object, place or idea as if it has human characteristics.

Pronoun – a word that takes the place of a noun (such as: I, she, them, it).

Propriety – having accepted standards of behaviour and morality.

Pseudoscience – ideas and practices mistakenly seen as being scientific.

Repetition – saying a word or phrase more than once, for effect.

Repress – to restrain or prevent something.

Sibilance – repetition of s sounds to create an effect.

Simile – a descriptive technique, using comparison to say one thing is 'like' or 'as' something else.

Sinful – having immoral behaviour.

Superlative – the most something can be (for example: biggest, highest, coldest).

Symbolise – when an object or colour represents a specific idea or meaning.

Tension – a feeling of anticipation, discomfort, or excitement.

Third-person narrative – a story told by a narrator who is not involved in the actual events.

Traditional – long-established or old-fashioned.

Troglodytic – primitive; like a prehistoric caveman.

Verb – a doing or action word.

Verb phrase – a group of words making up a verb.

Vice – immoral or criminal activity.

Vulgar – lacking good taste, refinement, and sophistication.

Zoomorphism – giving an object or emotion the characteristics of an animal.

Answers

the contrasting noun phrases 'evil influence' and 'new life' suggests that the murder case and the disappearance of Mr Hyde have made Dr Jekyll change his ways for the better.

Pages 10–11
Quick Test
1. Mid-conversation, a horrified expression suddenly appeared on his face before he closed the window and vanished from sight.
2. He heard Dr Jekyll cry out and believes someone else is now in the laboratory.
3. He saw a small man dash back into the laboratory.
4. Mr Hyde has poisoned himself, he appears to be wearing Dr Jekyll's clothes and there is a letter to Mr Utterson from Dr Jekyll.

Exam Practice
Analysis might include the following: the adverb 'seriously' shows the men know something is wrong and this is emphasised, as well as kept mysterious, by their 'silence'; the short clauses, pauses and repetition in Poole's speech make it seem disjointed to suggest his anxiety, and this is emphasised by the adjective 'afraid'; Poole's horror is shown through the phrase 'mottled pallor', while the vague noun 'thing' suggests mystery and monstrosity.

Pages 4–5
Quick Test
1. It looks sinister and neglected.
2. He ran into a girl, knocking her over, and continued to run across her body.
3. Dislike or hatred.
4. The cheque he produces is signed by someone else.
5. Dr Jekyll is not named to create mystery about who owns the building and who might be being blackmailed by Mr Hyde.

Exam Practice
Analysis might include the following: the adjective 'odd' suggests something unusual and this is emphasised by the adverb 'very'; the adjectives 'sick and white' show how strange and repulsive Mr Hyde seems, while the verb 'kill' emphasises the surprisingly extreme reaction that the doctor has; Mr Utterson's 'silence' and the metaphor 'weight of consideration' shows that there is a lot more to the story but Stevenson doesn't yet reveal those details.

Pages 12–13
Quick Test
1. It is written in the first person instead of the third person.
2. He believed he was mad.
3. He looked strange, his clothes were too big for him and he instantly repulsed Dr Lanyon.
4. Dr Lanyon can watch Mr Hyde take the potion or Mr Hyde can leave the house to take the potion.
5. The shock has made him ill and he believes he will soon die.

Exam Practice
Analysis might include the following: the adjective 'insane' shows that he thinks Dr Jekyll is mad and the noun 'colleague' (instead of, perhaps, the more informal 'friend') reminds the reader that they have had a disagreement; the noun phrase 'disgustful curiosity' shows that he is repulsed by Mr Hyde but wants to know more about him; the simile 'like a man restored from death' shows his shock at finding that Dr Jekyll is really Mr Hyde and this is emphasised through the exclamation mark and the use of a dash to create a dramatic pause in '– there stood Henry Jekyll!'.

Pages 6–7
Quick Test
1. Suspicious.
2. He gets angry and criticises Dr Jekyll's scientific work.
3. He is rude and secretive.
4. Mr Utterson lies that Dr Jekyll told him about Mr Hyde.
5. He says he can rid himself of Mr Hyde whenever he wants.

Exam Practice
Analysis might include the following: the adjective 'obnoxious' shows that he is concerned about the will, the verb 'fear' suggests that he worries about his friend and the reference to 'disgrace' shows how he is thinking about his friend's reputation; the metaphor 'turns me cold' shows his worries about his friend, the simile 'like a thief' suggests he is the victim of a criminal and calling him 'poor Harry' shows his sympathies, as well as their friendship (due to the informal version of Henry); the verb phrase 'heaved an irrepressible sigh' suggests a deep concern about Dr Jekyll's relationship with Mr Hyde.

Pages 14–15
Quick Test
1. His reputation.
2. Dr Jekyll changes into Mr Hyde while sleeping, without using the drug.
3. It takes a double dose, then the drug doesn't last as long and then he begins to run out (with the new supply not having any effect).
4. With none of the drug remaining, he knows he will never be able to change back into Dr Jekyll: he will become Mr Hyde forever.

Exam Practice
Analysis might include the following: at first Dr Jekyll is excited and curious, using adjective phrases such as 'something strange', 'indescribably new' and 'incredibly sweet'; the metaphor describing his blood as 'thin and icy' suggests his shock at the involuntary transformation into Mr Hyde, but use of 'exquisitely' suggests he is still fascinated by Mr Hyde and enjoys the sensations he feels when on his form; the refusal to use the first-person pronoun 'I' shows a wish to distance himself from Mr Hyde and this is later emphasised by the metaphor 'child of Hell' to portray how he is disgusted by Mr Hyde's evil and doesn't want to see him as his own creation.

Pages 8–9
Quick Test
1. It was an unprovoked attack on an old man and Mr Hyde stamped on him until he died.
2. Despite being in a run-down part of London, and despite Mr Hyde's appearance and behaviour, his lodgings are very nice.
3. It appears that Dr Jekyll has forged the letter claiming that Mr Hyde has made his escape.
4. Dr Lanyon becomes distressed when Dr Jekyll is mentioned; Dr Lanyon sends Mr Utterson an envelope that is not to be opened until after Dr Jekyll's death.

Exam Practice
Analysis might include the following: the adjective phrase 'deathly sick' suggests that the murder has horrified Dr Jekyll; the phrase 'forge for a murderer' suggests that Dr Jekyll has been corrupted by Mr Hyde and drawn into the murder case;

Pages 16–17

Quick Test

1. Much of the chapter is Mr Enfield's first-person, spoken account of meeting Mr Hyde.
2. Chapters 2 to 8.
3. Cliffhangers and the withholding of information.
4. Dr Lanyon in Chapter 9 and Dr Jekyll in Chapter 10 (and the letter in Chapter 9).
5. The first person makes the horror more immediate, as well as making it more believable by using intelligent, rational speakers.

Exam Practice

Analysis might include the following: Chapter 2 ends on a cliffhanger, showing Mr Utterson's fears for Dr Jekyll but giving no sense of how these might be resolved; to scare or disturb the reader, the list emphasises the depth of Dr Lanyon's horror and this is made more immediate through the first person; Dr Jekyll's first-person narrative helps the reader to understand his motivation and, as he is a scientist, his points seem rational or believable.

Pages 20–21

Quick Test

1. Prostitution.
2. Drug abuse.
3. The Government and the Church.
4. Both men are shocked to find out about Dr Jekyll's crimes; Utterson in particular links Mr Hyde to the lower classes. Stevenson is criticising how the middle classes tended to condemn vice and crime and relate it to the lower classes, ignorant of the fact that it was partly funded by middle class money.

Exam Practice

Analysis might include the following: despite being part of Dr Jekyll's middle class house, the door used by Mr Hyde is linked to the lower classes, symbolising how closely the two classes lived in society as well as the way social problems were easily ignored; the reference to 'tramps' suggests the poverty that was rife in the nineteenth century; the noun phrase 'sordid negligence' relates to the squalor of lower class areas, as well as their perceived lack of morality; disease was also a problem in lower class areas and this could be implied through the adjective 'blistered'; the way in which these social problems were largely ignored could also be suggested through the 'blind forehead', just as the lack of 'bell nor knocker' could represent how the higher classes were unwilling to help.

Pages 22–23

Quick Test

1. Unwritten rules about how to lives one's life: the importance of good appearance and behaviour, regular church attendance, moderation, sexual restraint and lower tolerance of crime.
2. Mr Utterson (and also Dr Lanyon).
3. Dr Jekyll appears respectable and belongs to a profession.
4. He yearns to indulge in vice; in the shape of Mr Hyde, we see his violent and corrupt side.

Exam Practice

Analysis might include the following: the noun phrase 'the acts of his life' highlights Mr Utterson's charitable nature; his behaviour at dinner seems very respectable as he is linked to being 'silent' rather than boastful or boisterous; the adjective 'austere' suggests a life of moderation and restraint, and this is emphasised by the way in which he tries to subdue ('mortify') his love of wine and doesn't visit the theatre despite finding it enjoyable.

Pages 24–25

Quick Test

1. The increase in realism was to make the novel seem more believable and, therefore, more frightening.

2. He is compared to monkeys several times to suggest he is a throwback to a lower form of life.
3. A false science, suggesting that a person's character could be assessed by their outward appearance.
4. Playing on society's expectations, Stevenson therefore makes Hyde look evil through his unusual face, shrunken body and strange walk.

Exam Practice

Analysis might include the following: the adjectives 'abnormal' and 'revolting' draw on physiognomy to suggest that Mr Hyde's appearance casts doubt on his 'character' and 'status in the world'; the adjective 'misbegotten' conveys a sense that there is something wrong with his appearance and this word is used to mean illegitimate, perhaps suggesting that Dr Lanyon is considering whether Mr Hyde is a product of sex outside wedlock (a sin in the nineteenth century); he is also compared to a 'creature' and there is a question about his 'origin', implying that Mr Hyde seems like some product of de-evolution.

Pages 26–27

Quick Test

1. Sinister settings, strange and frightening events, mystery and doubles.
2. The settings are nineteenth-century streets and buildings in London, and the frightening events are caused by science rather than the supernatural.
3. The solving of a mystery, a murder case, clues and evidence and Mr Utterson working alongside the police link to the detective genre; the fantastical exploration of scientific advances links to the science fiction genre.
4. The fear that society had become decadent and degenerate, losing its sense of morality and humanity.

Exam Practice

Analysis might include the following: Stevenson creates mystery for his reader by using aspects of the detective fiction genre; the stick is used as evidence of Hyde's crime but also provides a clue about his links to Jekyll; the Gothic horror genre is used to frighten the reader; this appears in the sinister settings, such as the death imagery in the 'swirling wreaths' of fog, the personification of the wind 'continually charging and routing' and the possible reference to Hell in the simile 'like the light of some strange conflagration'.

Pages 28–29

Quick Test

1. Focussing on the local shops, the area is clean, tidy and respectable.
2. The hallway is well-furnished and there is a large, roaring fire.
3. The costly furniture links to his wealth and this is also suggested by the exterior; the reference to it being 'ancient' and 'handsome' suggests Jekyll's reliability and respectability.
4. The windowless laboratory with its lack of light and suggestions of death and danger.

Exam Practice

Analysis might include the following: Dr Jekyll's respectability is mirrored by the appearance of the local shops, particularly in the adjective phrases 'freshly painted' and 'well-polished'; whilst the reference to the 'dingy' neighbourhood could symbolise how, like the shops, Dr Jekyll is superior to much of his area, it could also link to how he is drawn to corruption; the verb 'veiled' could also link to the way in which Dr Jekyll disguises his true self.

Answers

Pages 30–31
Quick Test
1. The description of the shops in Chapter 1 and the description of Dr Jekyll's house in Chapter 2.
2. It was over-populated, run-down, had suffered several cholera outbreaks and was known for prostitution, immigration and drunkenness.
3. Hell.
4. It is luxurious and displays good taste.

Exam Practice
Analysis might include the following: the personification of the building ('thrust forward') could link to Mr Hyde's aggressive behaviour; there are repeated references to normal things being absent ('no window, nothing but a door […] neither bell nor knocker') to suggest Hyde's secrecy and his degeneracy; his immorality is also conveyed through the adjectives 'sordid' and 'distained', while 'blistered' implies he is like a disease.

Pages 32–33
Quick Test
1. It suggests someone who is sensible, respectable and professional.
2. He looks honest, friendly and respectable.
3. Mr Utterson's comments that it was 'wild' and wonders whether he is being blackmailed over a past misdemeanour.
4. At first, he worries that Dr Jekyll is being blackmailed, then he suspects that he has helped Mr Hyde escape from the police, and in Chapter 8, he suspects Dr Jekyll has been murdered.

Exam Practice
Analysis might include the following: describing Dr Jekyll using the adjectives 'large, handsome' makes him seem like a good man, but the images of paleness and blackness suggests he has worries and secrets; Jekyll's morality, and regret for his association with Hyde, is suggested by the repetition of the verb phrase 'I swear to God'; the simile 'like some disconsolate prisoner' shows that Jekyll is unhappy and is trapped in some way, with his misery emphasised by the noun phrase 'infinite sadness'.

Pages 34–35
Quick Test
1. Mr Hyde is actually Dr Jekyll.
2. Dr Jekyll is insane.
3. Hiding or concealing them; feeling shame.
4. It creates more mystery but is also due to censorship at the time the novel was written.

Exam Practice
Analysis might include the following: the noun 'duplicity' links to the way Dr Jekyll hides the truth about himself (with 'duplicity' also meaning doubleness to show the different sides of his personality), but the verb 'committed' shows he accepts this as his way of life; the 'shipwreck' metaphor shows that his experiments bring about his downfall, he can't escape his disreputable desires or the temptation to be Mr Hyde; the repetition of the adverb 'truly' suggests Dr Jekyll is also being used by Stevenson as a representation of what Victorian society is really like; the contrasting feelings ('repugnance', 'welcome') show how Jekyll reacted to the release of his evil side in a positive way; again, the short sentence 'This, too, was myself' could be emphasising how Jekyll/Hyde is a representation of what Victorian society is really like.

Pages 36–37
Quick Test
1. The homophone suggests how Mr Hyde is used to conceal the truth about Dr Jekyll.
2. Monkeys, to link Mr Hyde to the idea of de-evolution.
3. He is referred to as bearing 'Satan's signature'.
4. Inside.

Exam Practice
Analysis might include the following: the repetition of the pronoun 'it' suggests Hyde is inhuman, while the adjective 'damned' implies his lack of morality and the noun 'juggernaut' (known in the nineteenth century as a huge wagon used as part of a Hindu festival) shows his power and aggression; comparing him to an ape suggests de-evolution to show his inhumanity, while the abstract noun 'fury' and the verb 'trampling' emphasise his uncontrollable aggression; the noun 'creature' and the adjectives 'abnormal' and 'misbegotten' suggest his inhumanity, with 'misbegotten' also implying that he might be of illegitimate birth to link to social prejudices of the Victorian era.

Pages 38–39
Quick Test
1. Better.
2. It is suggested that the good side of his nature is stronger and more dominant.
3. It is stronger and more aggressive.
4. The transformations become involuntary, it becomes more difficult for Jekyll to change back and Hyde begins to torment Jekyll, who grows weak compared with Hyde's strength.

Exam Practice
Analysis might include the following: the list of painful descriptions suggests that the experiment is unnatural and that Jekyll is releasing something terrible, but by referring to 'bones' and 'spirit', Stevenson suggests that this evil is a natural part of Jekyll; the abstract noun 'power' suggests the freedom that Hyde brings him but the metaphor 'fell into slavery' shows how this becomes addictive and controlling, which is also shown by the verb 'tempted'; Hyde's increased power and his ability to shock Jekyll appears in the metaphor 'spirit of Hell awoke in me and raged' and the uncontrollable violent instinct of Hyde is suggested by the adverb 'instantly'.

Pages 40–41
Quick Test
1. Shame and self-disgust, regret and guilt, and desperation.
2. The assault on the young girl and the brutal murder of Sir Danvers Carew.
3. Dr Lanyon and Mr Utterson.

Exam Practice
Analysis might include the following: the metaphor 'bind my honour' suggests that Jekyll is trying to make the right decision about Hyde and this is emphasised by the short sentence 'It is all at an end' (however, alternatively, we know that this doesn't last); the verb phrase 'brought on myself' shows he accepts responsibility and feels guilty for what he has done; the metaphor 'tasting delight' shows his pleasure in committing evil acts.

Pages 42–43

Quick Test

1. He seems miserable, serious, quiet and dull.
2. He is loveable, respectable, reliable and not judgemental.
3. He doesn't drink too much wine and he doesn't go to the theatre, despite enjoying both.
4. He hopes to find something he can use against Hyde in order to help Jekyll.

Exam Practice

Analysis might include the following: the adjective 'austere' represents Mr Utterson's modesty and respectability in line with Victorian values; the pun on 'hide and seek' shows Utterson's desire to help Jekyll by investigating Hyde, and this also links to his role as the novel's protagonist; the exclamation 'it's Hyde's!' shows how, in the third-person narrative, Utterson discovers things at the same time as the reader and his role of protagonist is also suggested by the imperative used.

Pages 44–45

Quick Test

1. He considers them unscientific nonsense.
2. He looks paler, thinner, balder and older.
3. The full reason for his initial disagreement with Jekyll, the reason for his later attitude to Jekyll and what has brought him close to death and the full explanation that Jekyll gives him after revealing that he is Hyde.
4. Because it makes Lanyon seem more reliable, it makes the events more realistic and therefore scarier.

Exam Practice

Analysis might include the following: the two verb phrases present Lanyon as lively and friendly; the 'death warrant' metaphor creates mystery about what has suddenly brought him close to death; the repetition of 'heard what I heard' creates simple finality that withholds key information and therefore creates mystery, while the metaphor 'my soul sickened' emphasises the horror of the transformation and the idea that it is unholy.

Pages 46–47

Quick Test

1. Enfield is wealthy, Poole is a servant.
2. Discretion, politeness and Christianity.
3. Suspicion and loathing.
4. Fear, anxiety and anger.

Exam Practice

Analysis might include the following: the adverb 'so' intensifies the ugliness of Hyde and the description of himself (Mr Enfield) sweating suggests fear or discomfort in Hyde's presence; the adjectives used to convey Poole's anxiety show his fears about Hyde and his suspicion that Jekyll has been murdered; the simile 'like ice' suggests how frighteningly monstrous Mr Hyde appears.

Pages 48–49

Quick Test

1. Appearance, behaviour and speech.
2. Satan, damned, Hell.
3. People have both good and evil inside them, but one impulse is stronger than the other.
4. The transformations become involuntary.

Exam Practice

Analysis might include the following: as well as the abstract noun 'cruelty', powerful adjectives are used to suggests Hyde's evil ('callous', 'vile', 'violent'); goodness is linked to honesty and light (the verbs 'open and brighten'), with the use of light possibly linking to biblical imagery, just as the word 'service' suggests Christian values; the verb 'gnashed' suggests evil is something bestial and the noun phrase 'devilish fury' links evil to Hell and sin.

Pages 50–51

Quick Test

1. Politeness, restraint, courtesy and a clear sense of right and wrong.
2. His speech and behaviour are aggressive; he lacks social politeness.
3. He avoids the theatre (and doesn't drink too much wine).
4. He wants to repress his desires but finds it too difficult.

Exam Practice

Analysis might include the following: the adjective 'modest' sums up the key characteristic of a respectable gentleman; respectability is expected of people who are 'well known', 'highly considered' or 'elderly' and this causes Jekyll to feel that he should repress his desires, referring to them negatively with the adjective 'undignified'; repression can be painful and this is shown through the verb 'tortured', and the desperation suggested by the abstract nouns 'throes' and 'longings'.

Pages 52–53

Quick Test

1. What the actual chemicals are and what his experiments have been.
2. Not being able to control Hyde.
3. He thinks he has full control over Hyde but is horrified when the transformations become involuntary.
4. He writes blasphemies over one of Jekyll's religious books.

Exam Practice

Analysis might include the following: talking to Lanyon, Hyde – although this might be Jekyll's scientific arrogance emerging – presents Jekyll's scientific discoveries as exciting (the repetition of 'new') and advantageous (the abstract nouns 'fame and power'); science is made frightening and strange through the verbs 'melt and alter', with the traditional colour symbolism of 'black' also implying it is immoral or unholy; science is presented as dangerous through the verb phrases 'slowly losing hold' and 'slowly incorporated' to show Jekyll's loss of identity and this is emphasised by the contrasting adjectives 'better' and 'worse' to show that science causes his downfall.

Pages 54–55

Quick Test

1. He knew his experiment could bring about an amazing discovery but also that it could kill him.
2. The letter is linked to a murder case so it would be dishonest not to hand it to the police. However, it incriminates his friend. When he realises it could be a forgery, there is the added dimension that Utterson himself is aiding Hyde's escape by keeping the letter secret.
3. Death is initially presented literally, as Hyde could be hanged for the murder of Sir Danvers Carew. Death then becomes metaphorical as Jekyll begins to lose his own identity to Hyde and ultimately realises that he will never be able to change back.

Exam Practice

Analysis might include the following: the noun 'debate' shows that Jekyll's decision was not a easy one, with the words 'inducements' and 'tempted' showing the excitement of possible scientific discoveries but being contrasted with the words 'alarms' and 'trembling' to show his fear of the possible consequences; Jekyll's awareness that he made the wrong decision is shown in the nouns 'punishment' and 'calamity'; the 'doom' metaphor shows that he realises the fatal consequence of his decision.

Answers

3. Quotations give you more opportunities to do specific AO2 analysis.

Exam Practice

Ideas might include the following: his unwillingness to let Mr Utterson help and the way he deliberately obscures the truth; the way in which he presents himself as having a kind interest in the life of Edward Hyde; his disagreement and frustration with Dr Lanyon; his charitable works and sociability when he temporarily rids himself of Mr Hyde, compared to his later seclusion.

Pages 56–57

Quick Test

1. The contrasts between Jekyll and Hyde, and all the other contrasting images in the novel, foreshadow the idea that Jekyll and Hyde are actually the same person.
2. The front looks friendly, wealthy and well-kept; the back looks unwelcoming, sinister and neglected.
3. The streets outside are dirty and linked to poverty and immorality, but the interior is luxurious, well-decorated and respectable.

Exam Practice

Ideas might include the following: duality is presented through the differences between Jekyll and Hyde with the former being 'tall' and the latter being a 'dwarf', the negative connotations of which also contrast with the word 'master' to suggest how Jekyll has greater respect and reputation; the phrase 'dual nature' asserts that duality is a natural feature of human identity and this is explored through the contrasting nouns 'good and ill'; duality is also explored as a battle for dominance, rather than a peaceful coexistence, through the verb 'contended'.

Pages 62–63

Quick Test

1. Understanding of the whole text, specific analysis and terminology, awareness of the relevance of context, a well-structured essay and accurate writing.
2. Planning focusses your thoughts and allows you to produce a well-structured essay.

Pages 66–67 and 72–73

Exam Practice

Use the mark scheme below to self-assess your strengths and weaknesses. Work up from the bottom, putting a tick by things you have fully accomplished, a ½ by skills that are in place but need securing and underlining areas that need particular development. The estimated grade boundaries are included so you can assess your progress towards your target grade.

Pages 68–69

Quick Test

1. Understanding of the whole text, specific analysis and terminology, awareness of the relevance of context, a well-structured essay and accurate writing.
2. Planning focusses your thoughts and allows you to produce a well-structured essay.
3. Quotations give you more opportunities to do specific AO2 analysis.

Exam Practice

Ideas might include the following: Dr Jekyll's good reputation referred to in Chapter 10 and Chapter 6; Mr Utterson's wish to help save Dr Jekyll's reputation; Dr Jekyll's own worries about his reputation after the murder of Sir Danvers Carew; Dr Jekyll's wish to maintain his reputation whilst indulging his desires and the ways in which this links to Stevenson's ideas about Victorian society.

Grade	AO1 (12 marks)	AO2 (12 marks)	AO3 (6 marks)	AO4 (4 marks)
6–7+	A convincing, well-structured essay that answers the question fully. Quotations and references are well-chosen and integrated into sentences. The response covers the whole novel.	Analysis of the full range of Stevenson's methods. Thorough exploration of the effects of these methods. Accurate range of subject terminology.	Exploration is linked to specific aspects of the novel's contexts to show a detailed understanding	Consistent high level of accuracy. Vocabulary and sentences are used to make ideas clear and precise.
4–5	A clear essay that always focusses on the exam question. Quotations and references support ideas effectively. The response refers to different points in the novel.	Explanation of Stevenson's different methods. Clear understanding of the effects of these methods. Accurate use of subject terminology.	References to relevant aspects of context show a clear understanding.	Good level of accuracy. Vocabulary and sentences help to keep ideas clear.
2–3	The essay has some good ideas that are mostly relevant. Some quotations and references are used to support the ideas.	Identification of some different methods used by Stevenson to convey meaning. Some subject terminology.	Some awareness of how ideas in the novel link to its context.	Reasonable level of accuracy. Errors do not get in the way of the essay making sense.

Answers